WILHELM STEKEL

THE LIFE STORY OF A PIONEER PSYCHOANALYST

PLAQUE IN COMMEMORATION OF DR. STEKEL'S
SIXTIETH ANNIVERSARY

The Autobiography of

WILHELM STEKEL

THE LIFE STORY OF A PIONEER PSYCHOANALYST

Edited by

EMIL A. GUTHEIL, M.D.

With an Introduction by

MRS. HILDA STEKEL, London

Fools they that die for some dead past in vain!
All he once lost, the wise man wins again . . .
WILHELM STEKEL

LIVERIGHT PUBLISHING CORPORATION
NEW YORK

TABLE OF CONTENTS

v

11537

Contents

CHAPTER IX

CHIEF OF THE ACTIVE-ANALYTIC CLINIC

CHAPTER X

A REFUGEE FROM THE NAZIS

LIST OF ILLUSTRATIONS

PREFACE

by

EMIL A. GUTHEIL, M.D.

WHEN AFTER Wilhelm Stekel's death, his wife, Mrs. Hilda Stekel, bestowed upon me the honor of editing his *Autobiography,* I soon realized what she meant when she intimated that the manuscript had been written in unusual haste. Much of the material was disorganized. Nevertheless, to one who had long been versed in the distinguished psychologist's method and who was familiar with many of the details of his personal life, the dramatic force and beauty of his story was consistently apparent.

Wilhelm Stekel was a pioneering psychoanalyst whose prodigious intuition and medical skill had permitted him to compile, study, and interpret the case histories of thousands of patients. When he felt that the sands of his life were running low, he wanted to leave his own "case history" to posterity, particularly to the coming generations of psychotherapists. He was in a hurry. Cataclysmic World War II events were besetting him; a grave illness he well understood was hewing at his

11

gaunt, proud figure. Calmly, but with intense speed, he prepared his record.

There is no doubt that in his decision to write his autobiography Stekel was influenced by Jean Jacques Rousseau's *Confessions*. He had always deplored the fact that in world literature only a few autobiographies were sufficiently intimate and frank for the analyst-reader to evaluate the personality of the author involved. Stekel admired the rare courage and brilliant insight of the French philosopher so much that he made a thought-provoking psychological analysis of Rousseau's personality through his writings.[1]

Stekel hoped that his own autobiography would be used in a similar way as a source for analytic research. As a brain specialist might will his own brain to medical investigators, so did the author of the ten-volume work on *Disorders of the Instincts and Emotions* wish to leave the account of his own instincts and emotions for the benefit of the students of psychoanalysis.

Such was the way of the real Stekel. When the great teacher and practitioner was no longer able to instruct in lecture halls or clinics, when he could no longer introduce live patients to demonstrate the intricacies of psychotherapy, he took the one available subject—himself—and posed it in the nude, stripped of every conventional reserve.

In his account of himself Stekel tried hard to be unbiased; however, his success in this respect was little more than that of some of his own patients who sub-

---

[1] "Jean Jacques Rousseau. Analysis of an Exhibitionist." Chapter XXV of Stekel's *Psychosexueller Infantilismus*, Urban & Schwarzenberg, Vienna, 1922.

mitted prepared autobiographical data to him. He was not able to duplicate the vein of the masochistic exhibitionist Rousseau, whose memoirs were extraordinarily revealing because they constituted a form of self-exposure and self-chastisement. The student of psychoanalysis can see in Stekel's notes how many of his own complexes remained obscure to him, can detect his unresolved narcissism, his overcompensated feelings of inadequacy; will smile when he reads that the man who was a master in ferreting out other people's repressions believed that he had hardly any himself. Then there is Stekel's failure to recognize his affect-heavy attitude toward his teacher, Freud, upon whom he tried in vain to transfer his own father-complex.

But the analytical reader will also appreciate in Stekel the great clinician and psychologist, the erudite man of letters, the warm-hearted lover of the arts. To the mind of this editor come the words of Conrad Ferdinand Meyer, the Swiss poet whom Stekel liked to quote:

"I'm not a book that's filled with clever fiction;
I am a human heart with all its contradiction." [2]

Stekel was both persevering and impatient; shrewd and naive. Was it an accident that it was he who discovered the principle of bipolarity of human emotions? [3]

Stekel's *Autobiography* is more than a personal narrative. It breathes the air of old Vienna and recaptures the charm of the cosmopolitan Europe that was. It

---

[2] "Ich bin kein ausgeklügelt Buch;
   Ich bin ein Mensch mit seinem Widerspruch."
[3] This psychological phenomenon was rediscovered by the Swiss, Eugene Bleuler, who termed it "ambivalence," the name by which Freud introduced it into psychoanalysis.

throws an interesting light upon an early phase of the psychoanalytic movement in which the author played a prominent part. He describes the intimate gatherings of Freud, Alfred Adler, and himself where they discussed ways and means to introduce psychoanalysis to medicine. Later as co-editor with Freud of *Zentralblatt für Psychoanalyse* he writes of the search for landmarks in a new field, of the discouragements and disagreements, and finally of world-wide acceptance of their theories.

The editor has tried to select with discrimination those details of Stekel's intimate life which he deemed essential for the understanding of the author's personality. Whenever the blue pencil has been wielded, it has been done with full respect for the author's text and theme.

In the *Autobiography,* in addition to photos, various members of Stekel's school are briefly introduced as well as miscellaneous biographical material presented by the editor.

INTRODUCTORY NOTE

by

Mrs. Hilda Stekel
London

My husband, Wilhelm Stekel, ended his life voluntarily in London on June 25, 1940. Thus, suffering humanity lost one of its great healers. In his farewell letter, my husband asked me to publish his *Autobiography*. He suggested that I shorten the manuscript and write a last chapter dealing with his illness and death.

The publication of this *Autobiography*, a matter so close to my heart, was delayed by the intricate events of world history. I am, therefore, pleased and deeply touched because my husband's last wish is now fulfilled; and I am most grateful to the *American Journal of Psychotherapy* and to the Liveright Publishing Corporation for their readiness to honor the deceased by publishing his last work.[1]

Within the covers of this small volume is the essence of Wilhelm Stekel's work and personality. The book

---

[1] Parts of Wilhelm Stekel's *Autobiography* appeared in eight installments in the *American Journal of Psychotherapy*, New York, 1947-1949.—*The Editor.*

also renders a service to the public, to the author's many pupils, followers, readers, colleagues, and patients in all parts of the world by informing them of the real reasons for his suicide, the motives of which have been misinterpreted by some newspapers and scientific journals and by many individuals.

I asked Dr. Emil A. Gutheil of New York City to undertake the difficult task of revising my husband's *Autobiography*. I felt that I was too close to the subject to treat it with the desired editorial impartiality. Dr. Gutheil, as one of Dr. Stekel's first pupils and most faithful friends, appeared best suited for the assignment. I thank him on this occasion for his splendid achievement.

Dr. Stekel began writing the story of his life while he was still in Vienna. He had finished his *Technique of Analytical Psychotherapy*[2] and felt an urge to conclude his literary work with an autobiography. He hoped that by publishing a frank and unbiased account of his own life he might be able to contribute some constructive ideas to the problems of education, mental hygiene, and the prophylaxis of nervous disorders.

Three days before the war started I returned from Norway to England. I had visited my daughter, Dr. Erica Wendelbo, who had gone to Norway after we had fled from Vienna, and married there. I joined my husband who was in the country at this time. Writing his autobiography offered my husband a welcome stimula-

---

[2] *Verlag für Medizin,* Hans Huber, Berne, Switzerland, 1938. English translation: Norton and Co., New York, 1941. At present, out of print.—*The Editor.*

tion and helped him to weather the tense atmosphere of these first weeks after the outbreak of the war.

Our plans were unsettled. We had contemplated a long stay in the country. However, when my husband finished his autobiography he could not endure country life any longer and returned to London. He stayed at the hotel where we had lived upon our arrival in England. Today, I regret that we had no chance to have a home and that it was his fate to die "homeless" in more than one sense.

I could not accompany him to London because I was convalescing after a serious operation and was in poor physical and mental condition. My aged mother and I lived with a friend, Miss Elna Kallenberg, now Mrs. F. L. Lucas, in Cambridge. Elna's kindness and companionship were indeed helpful as we strove to endure the depressing and uncertain lot of refugees. I am fulfilling my husband's wish when I thank our "Guardian Angel" in this way.

I also take this opportunity to thank Mr. Fritz Mumenthaler of Berne, Switzerland, who, by storing my husband's precious library, saved it from destruction. I owe it to this noble-minded man, who previously was unknown to us, that my husband's library is now available to me. Incidentally, it was Elna and our young friend, Dr. Karl Merkel, who first rescued the library by sorting out the enormous amount of books we had and sending them to Switzerland. In Vienna, all of Stekel's books and manuscripts were destroyed as were the books of Freud, Adler, and many other authors.

My husband was happy when he was able to resume

his practice and continue his other activities in London. The uneventful months of the "phony war" found him in relatively good spirits. He borrowed music from a lending library and spent many hours at a piano which belonged to the hotel. It was remarkable how easily he was able to adapt himself to circumstances, and how patiently he endured the limitations imposed upon him by his diabetes and prostatic trouble. His vital energies, though, were reduced noticeably by the harrowing experience of emigration as well as by an acute intestinal disease which attacked him shortly after his arrival in London. He aged rapidly thereafter. His diabetes grew worse and he was forced to take insulin to keep it under control.

One day, in February or March, 1940, I was called urgently to the hotel. I found my husband in bed, completely apathetic. I was told that he was in a hypoglycemic coma, probably because he had injected too large a dose of insulin. I was surprised that he refused the orange juice we offered and that it had to be forced into him. Soon the glucose had its effect and he recovered. I suspect that this was his first suicide attempt— made with conscious or unconscious intent. He had at that time diabetic gangrene of the foot which troubled him a great deal. Those who know how much my husband loved long walks will appreciate the hardship such suffering brought upon him. As a physician he knew, of course, what this condition meant.

In April, Norway was overrun by the Nazis, and I worried about my daughter who lived in Elverum where the first battles took place. My husband was very much upset about reports of the Nazi occupation of this area, and his foot condition grew markedly worse. When, after two anxious months, we received the news that Erica was alive, our relief was wonderful.

My husband was unshaken in his belief that England would be spared from the ravages of war. Apparently this was the optimism his weakened organism employed to ward off the prospect of harmful excitement. Even after Belgium and Holland had fallen and the war came closer to our door, he did not want to recognize the impending danger and felt quite "secure." He was too ill to move out of London, anyway.

At that time my mother and I started on a hectic period of wanderings. We were forced to change quarters constantly. It was a time when England proceeded with the internment of foreigners; many areas were declared "restricted," others "protected," and evacuation on a large scale was carried out. England prepared for an invasion. In those stormy days I felt keenly what it meant to be without a home and a homeland.

When I visited my husband in June, I found him physically and mentally in poor condition. His foot was much worse. The collapse of France shocked him profoundly. He loved France. He could not bear the thought that such a country should be enslaved. With the fall of France, serious personal anxieties also appeared. Both of Dr. Stekel's children lived in France. He was particularly worried about his son, Eric, a renowned musician and conductor, who had been drafted into a work battalion and who, he thought, was in danger of being shot.

When I saw my husband then, I was painfully impressed by his haggard, yellow-hued countenance.

Our friend, Mrs. Mundy Castle, who saw him at that time, described him as follows: "He was dressed carefully in grey and white. The grey of his suit toned with the silver of his hair and his well-trimmed beard. The effect was almost ethereal. One could not help looking at this old man astounded, almost with awe, for he was a shadow of his former self. He had passed into a new dimension. A sense of stillness and a sense of resolution emanated from him, which are difficult to describe. He had reached a new composure. Whatever he was thinking was not of here and now; he was looking towards another place. Yet of all the men I had seen in him, here he was, his truest self. Among the various things he said to me, small things, there are three I remember best: 'The answer to life is work.' 'It is joy, the joy of life that is lacking in the world of today. The joy of life is the answer.' And the third, 'It is all done by love.' When a week later a friend of mine, whom I wished to be his patient, rang him up at his hotel, he put the receiver down, saying, 'He is dead.' "

On the day I visited my husband, Prime Minister Chamberlain was overthrown and Winston Churchill took over the reins of the British Government. When I commented on this new situation, my husband surprised me with the remark, "I am not interested in politics." I did not understand at that time that these changes did not mean much to him any more. In the course of our conversation he complained that his foot disturbed him at night and that the thought of his family deprived him of his sleep which had always been excellent. He was unable to find a book that could divert him. When I offered to stay with him in London he opposed me vigorously. He said that he needed rest and that since I myself was too restless at night, I would only disturb him. When we parted I cried bitterly. This was the last time I saw him. Four days later my husband took his life.

Dr. Stekel was well-liked by the hotel guests. They esteemed the sick old man who never complained, who never bewailed his past, and who seemed to have made a complete adjustment to the new life. They were upset by the tragedy. According to their report, on Monday morning my husband went to his doctor to get his regular short-wave treatment. He was in good spirits. When he returned, he said that because of his diabetes his doctor had ordered him to take nothing but tea for one full day. He asked not to be disturbed in the afternoon as he wished to remain in bed. In this way he took precautions against possible obstruction of his plan. When on Tuesday he was not seen in the lobby, the hotel manager grew worried. The door of his room was forced open and my husband was found in bed—lifeless.

Later, I received an envelope containing a brief note and a few pound bills which my husband had left for me. The note stated that I would probably need some cash.

All the other envelopes containing farewell letters were held by the coroner until after the inquest. I spent two days in painful and uncertain speculation as to what might have induced my husband to make this fatal decision. Then I received the letters. I found that he had written three letters to me, one to his physician, and one to each of his patients. He also left a letter which was deeply touching. He expressed his thanks to

England for her hospitality and his belief in the greatness of the country and its final victory. He asked all his friends, pupils, and patients to forgive him for letting them down but that he could not go on.

From the long letter which, unfortunately, was kept by the coroner, I am quoting only the few lines which were published by the newspapers:

"I am passing away like a warrior. Guns and cannons are only temporary. The greatness for which England stands will put right all wrongs."

I learned from the letters he had written on three consecutive days that he had planned his suicide several months before taking action. He had always hoped for a change in his physical condition, but now, because of the decline of his health, his life had become unbearable. The agonies Freud had to endure before his passing in 1939 were a warning to him. He asked me to forgive him. He urged me to go on living and to continue his work as an analyst. He also mentioned that his subscription at the lending library was still valid and that I should make full use of it. Nothing touched me more than this trifle which he did not overlook in the last solemn moments of his life. I believe it proves beyond doubt the calmness and clarity of mind that was his at the time. Strange as it may seem, according to the laboratory examination my husband used aspirin to poison himself.

Dr. Stekel was a master of the art of living and a man who loved freedom above all else. He was impatient with annoying people (except patients) and did not want to put up with the little vexations of life. He often left a theatre after the first act if he did not like the performance. It was, therefore, entirely consistent with his usual behavior that he "walked off" when life became a burden to him. He was a realist, and, as a physician, he was aware of the fact that with his diabetes, his prostatic disorder and his arteriosclerosis becoming more severe, his future held no joy. What he dreaded most was that he might become too helpless to end it all. When he found his time was up, he bowed out gracefully like an ancient philosopher.

All this occurred at a critical time for all England. Everybody was concerned with his own worries. Thus, only a few people knew of the cremation of my husband which took place at Golder's Green. His ashes were spread at the Garden of Rest. No memorial tablet was erected.

The dailies which reported the suicide quoted the verdict of the inquest that it was an act committed by an "unbalanced mind." This sounds like grim irony in the face of the details mentioned above. Stekel's *Autobiography*, therefore, will serve as a justification and a vindication of a great man whose work was often as much misunderstood as was the motive for his death.

HILDA STEKEL

London, November, 1948

WILHELM STEKEL

THE LIFE STORY OF A PIONEER PSYCHOANALYST

Chapter One

CHILDHOOD

★

*In life as in the practice of a
physician—the first steps decide.*
—LICHTENBERG

IN UNDERTAKING to write my biography, I am fully conscious of the difficulty of the task. Even the intention to
keep close to the truth unconditionally, and not to be
hampered by prejudice or discretion, represents a con-
flicting situation. I feel that I have to overcome serious
inhibitions in order to transform Goethe's maxim,
"Poetry and Truth," into the more sober maxim,
"Truth without Poetry." Psychoanalysis has taught us
to distrust our memories. Freud proved that there are
screen memories, pictures of an apparently harmless
nature behind which vitally important experiences lie
hidden. How can one separate the chaff from the wheat,
how distinguish false memories from accurate ones?

It is strange that most people know so little about
their own childhood. Even more strange, most parents
are blind to the experiences of their children. A person
who is blind to his own childhood wears psychic blind-

27

ers which prevent him from seeing many important qualities of his children, especially those qualities and events he himself has repressed.

The first child seen by the magnifying glass of psychoanalysis was "Little Hans" [1] whose initial conflicts Freud described in detail as the phobia of a boy of five years. It is wonderful to read how the youngster had to fight his first internal battle between craving and inhibition, between instincts and morals. Every week his parents took him to Freud and discussed with the master the events and the results of their observations. Thus, the boy had what may be called his first psychoanalysis.

Sixteen years later a young man came to Freud and introduced himself with the words, "I am 'Little Hans.' Yesterday I read the story of my childhood. It will interest you to know that I have forgotten everything except one insignificant detail. I have even forgotten that I came every week to see you."

This happens to most people. Therefore, exceptions such as myself, who remember their first experiences clearly should enlighten humanity about the true nature of a child.

There are many biographies and "confessions." You may ask whether it is absolutely necessary or desirable for me to supply the public with another life story. My book is unique in that it offers the confessions of a psychoanalyst who has placed his experiences beneath the magnifying glass of psychology in an attempt to induce important conclusions upon the pressing current prob-

---

[1] "Analyse der Phobie eines fünfjährigen Knaben" (Analysis of a Phobia in a Five-year-old Boy), *Coll. Papers*, Vol. VIII, pp. 127-264 (German edition).

lems of education. In my book, *A Primer for Mothers*,[2] I presented the fundamentals of a prophylactic education. The success of that book which has, in twenty-two languages, appealed to the minds and hearts of mothers, seems to show beyond question that it filled a gap.

From the numerous existing autobiographies I would comment only on Rousseau's *Confessions;* for all the other autobiographies, and many autobiographic novels, neglect the first impressions of childhood and lack the truth regarding the important problems of sex life. I understand the reluctance these writers have of standing naked before the curious and leering eyes of misunderstanding observers. Many have left sincere diaries with the injunction that they should be published after a certain time. Alas, in spite of the explicit instructions in the last will of the authors, these books were never published. Sometimes they were destroyed, sometimes they were buried in some locked library.

I know people will vilify me and cast stones at me. But I know, too, that I am not different from other people, that I am perhaps better than some, that I show strength in not retouching the photo of my life or presenting myself as better than I am. Goethe once said: "I never heard of a crime I couldn't have committed myself under certain circumstances." What illuminating words! Perhaps we are all more or less alike.

EARLY CHILDHOOD

I am the third living child of my parents, and was born in Boyan, Bukovina. In those days it was Austrian

2 Macaulay Co., New York, 1931.

territory, but it now belongs to Rumania.[3] Preceding me
were my brother, six years my senior, and my sister,
three years my senior. Four children died before the
birth of my brother. My grandmother was still alive. I
can picture her wrinkled, wise, and jocular face and her
active figure. My grandfather had been dead a long
time. His first name was Perez and his ancestors were
refugees from Spain.

How far back do my memories go? I know that we
moved from the little village of Boyan to Czernowitz
(Cernauti) , the capital of Bukovina. It was during the
first years of my life. About my earliest youth I know
much from the stories of my mother. My nurse was a
Ukrainian peasant, Marysia, of whom I know that she
had frequent spells of bad temper. My first language was
Ukrainian. It was often said that Marysia had transferred her wild temperament to me. My parents were
kindhearted; I have seldom seen them angry, but Marysia used to tear her clothes and throw glasses to the floor.
Among other things it made her furious when I composed senseless rhymes.

While I should not like to decide whether or not a
nurse is capable of transferring a part of her temperament to the child she suckles, I am convinced that she
can give the child an impressive object lesson in tan-
trums. My mother was certain that my wild temperament came from Marysia's milk. The nurse remained
with us long after I had been weaned. However, I have
no conscious recollection of this nurse; what I know of
her is derived from what my mother told me. I am not
so fortunate as Tolstoi, who, in his book, *Earliest Child-*

---

3 Bukovina is now in the U.S.S.R.—*The Editor.*

hood, wrote that he remembered the time when, as an infant, he was wrapped so tightly in bandages that he was unable to move. He cried and wished to be free. He was certain that this was his first and most vivid memory.

Do we not see in this memory the whole later Tolstoi? All his life he felt the shackles of law, the manacles of marriage, the bondage of the proprieties, and he tried to free himself. In his story, he remembers the whole room resounded with his crying; and did he not later fill the whole world with his din? He realized that he had condensed a number of recollections in this one characteristic picture. What did he do at the end of his life? He looked for freedom; he left his family and his estate; he died as a free man at a railway station in an out-of-the-way corner of the Russian Empire. It was his last station indeed. What he yearned for as a child and could not attain because he was swaddled in diapers, he could achieve at a time when the wings of death were rushing around him, and bringing back to him what he considered his first memory.

My own first recollection is less dramatic. It seems indifferent, without emotion and without importance. How could it linger in my memory if my inner-self had not been strongly stirred?

I see the house in which we lived after moving from Boyan. It stands at the crossroads; there is a simple cart in which my grandmother is sitting; after a short visit with us she was going back to Boyan. Now I see with my mind's eye how my mother gives her a lemon to suck for refreshment on the trip.

I would explain this memory as the jealousy of the

little boy because his mother has neglected him in the presence of the grandmother. Indeed, I have a second memory that may confirm this supposition. Grandmother died. Mother returned in excitement from the funeral. She told how, after Grandmother's death, neighbors had ransacked the dead woman's house and stolen many objects. My feeling was a mixture of surprise and malignant joy.

Before this, something happened that determined my whole life. I visited my grandmother in Boyan, walked in the "main street," that is, the one street of the village. A little girl called to me. She gave me a bunch of cherries and asked me to play with her. We played the favorite game of children, "father and mother." My playmate was partly the hostess and partly the servant. I alternated between the role of a host and that of a visitor. (Now there is a gap in my mind.) Nearby is an improvised shed which I remember distinctly. Carpenters had placed boards in such a way as to form a pyramid-like structure. They had nailed the boards together in order to provide a shelter against the rain. We entered the shed and looked cautiously around us. Then we continued to play "father and mother," and this time we enjoyed the physical side of our "marriage."

How did the knowledge of this natural procedure come into my brain? Was it an inherited instinct, or the imitation of something observed in my parents' home? I cannot decide, but I know that the realization we had done something forbidden came to us both. It was already dark. We crept shyly away from our hiding place and looked around. Did a peasant pass? Did we hear voices of wayfarers? This part is hazy, but I visualize us leaving the shack hand in hand and walking up to our elders. They must have been astonished that we came home so late.[4]

I cannot remember any more of my relationship with this girl. I was probably two-and-a-half years old. (Incidentally, thirty years later, I was the physician of this same girl. She was married and had two children. I asked her whether she remembered our play, and I was astonished to hear that it had completely disappeared from her memory. She only recalled that my older brother once knocked her down and she showed me a little scar which resulted from this assault. A distinct "screen memory.")

Did I see my little wife a second time? I do not know. I see myself riding home in a simple cart in which there are many grown-ups. I am entrusted to the care of a man during the trip which requires one hour. I have a small wooden flute like those which peasants make. I try to play on it. The flute falls from my hand to the road. I cry bitterly. The carriage stops. Some of the men go down to look for the flute. The passengers are in a hurry. They shout to the driver, "Go on! Go on!" The cart rumbles and creaks over the dusty road. I sadly look back. My crying has been in vain. The hot sun presses the tears against my cheeks. The wonderful flute is lost forever.

How can I learn why this scene is engraved so deeply in my memory? Was the flute the symbol of the lost

---

[4] This experience, together with similar experiences of his friends, was later used as a basis for Stekel's first medical paper on the *Sex Life in Children*. It was published independently of Freud who later quoted from it in one of his early works on infantile sexuality.—*The Editor*.

girl? Does the loss represent the loss of my sweetheart? Have I taken this scene from the treasure-house of my memories and kept it because it reminds me of the beautiful words, "Everything that passes by is only a smile"?

Do we really know what processes occur in a child's brain? Most of us forget our own childhood except for a few scattered images. What Freud calls "repression" seems to represent a purely protective function of our psychic life. To live means to forget things which make life painful. One of my patients who suffered from agoraphobia confessed to me that she had often played improperly with her son. The boy had shared her bed from infancy until some time after puberty. The woman abruptly stopped having sexual intimacies with her son and behaved irreproachably thenceforth. She tried to erase the effects of her earlier mistakes by giving her son an excellent education. Following her recovery I heard nothing of the patient or her son for a long time. One day a twenty-one-year-old man, the patient's son, came to see me in my office. He suffered from depressions and one of my experienced assistants took over his treatment, after I informed the doctor of the salient facts I knew from the mother. My assistant and I waited tensely for weeks and months to see whether our patient would recall his embarrassing childhood experiences; he did not.

It is hard to determine whether he did not wish or was unable to recall. The analysis suggested that he re-lived these early impressions in his day-dreams and that it was apparently this factor that was responsible for his inability to concentrate and for his depressions. However,

when the analysis came close to the problem in question, the patient displayed the "flight reflex" and discontinued the treatment.

But to return to the "central character" and good
chronological order. From my first memories emerge a
lot of irrelevant ones. I know I was not a model child.
I was wild, stubborn, defiant; I was a problem child and
very difficult to bring up. My mother had a remarkable
principle: each human being must have a time in his
life in which he can storm out his temperament. She
read this sentence in some book or she heard it in the
theater, but it was her principle, and she used to say,
"It's better my child storms now than later."

Marysia had gone, and my poor mother had the whole
burden of the naughty boy; but she never lost her patience, and I was never physically punished by her.

After the death of my grandmother we moved to a
place where many houses stood in a circle around a big
court; nearby were large lawns and gardens. There
were a lot of "good-for-nothing" boys and girls; we liked
to climb over the fence into a big orchard which was not
used, and therefore neglected and growing wild, and
this orchard was our playground. Usually we played cops
and robbers, but also many less innocent games and we
had many talks on the riddle of sex. The story of the
innocence of children is a fairy tale. Whoever insists
on the truth of this fairy tale does not know children,
for when not directly controlled by adults, they soon
show their true nature.

I do not remember the first day I went to school (a
milestone for every child). I was so engrossed in my
daydreams and games that school and learning were

intensely boring. I remember some teachers, some pranks, some wanton talks with other boys; in class, I did not pay attention to the lectures. The results were miserable. I had the worst possible marks and frequently was "kept in" to learn my lessons.

Suppose that a teacher or a doctor had examined me at that time; he would have stated that I was not fit for school and, perhaps, that I was a backward child. I have often had the opportunity to console parents who complained about their children's bad marks in the elementary school. Many "slow" children live in a world of fantasy which is stronger than anything else. The world of fairy tales gives them more pleasure than that of reality. I want to emphasize that I was not the only naughty child; there were dozens and dozens like myself. Later they became virtuous citizens; some were successes, some were failures.

BOOKS

We moved again. Now I attended a Protestant, co-educational school, which was known as a model school. My teachers were kind, the spirit of the school was excellent, the teaching was stimulating. The children were from a higher social stratum than were my earlier classmates. There were none of the roughnecks of the former period.

I was able to read very early, but I had never read stories. But now I had a delightful experience. I found a children's book. I can visualize the picture on the title page: a powerful giant, a little boy, and a church bell. I see myself lying on the couch and devouring line

after line with my cheeks burning. That day I discovered my "reading ego," and my passion for reading has
remained throughout my life. My parents used my
voracious reading as a means of restraining me when I
ran wild. When visitors came I was, as a rule, a nuisance and a troublemaker. I wanted to be the center of
attention, and tormented visitors with thousands of
questions; but if I had a book with illustrations, I
looked at the pictures, let my fantasy drift, and hours
would pass by in perfect silence. When I accompanied
my parents on a visit to friends, my first question directed to our hosts was, "Have you any books with illustrations?" When my wish was granted I did not molest
the adults any more.

I must mention here that the games with the boys
continued, although in a different form; we now were
a gang, and our captain was a boy of fourteen. We had
to obey like soldiers. And yet I must say that the interest in books was stronger than anything else. My brother,
who was six years my senior, had the same passion. He
already had a small library; the books were in a locked
bookcase; I could see them through the glass. I remember having had an idea that if my brother should die I
would inherit all these beautiful books.

I tried to get books at any price. I borrowed them
from other boys, and sometimes I bought the cruel
books about Indians. Most of them were dirty and torn.
They had passed through many hands. Usually I identified myself with the hero, and in my daydreams I was a
great man, the leader of an army (the Austrian army, of
course), fighting against the armies of the Czar and
killing thousands of enemies. At this time an actress

lived in our house, and sometimes I received complimentary tickets (standing room) from her. But I do not remember the plays. I only know how sorry I felt when the theatre was empty. I counted every visitor and was glad when a new one arrived. I wanted to create my own plays. Our theatre was the porch of the Greek Orthodox Church which stood in the center of a vast meadow surrounded by a fence. Everything was improvised, and I invariably played the villain or the robber captain.

I am sorry to say that I also wanted to be a real robber; sometimes all my wild instincts overwhelmed me. I stole money from my father's pocket, bought candies and shared them with the gang. We caught innocent boys and gave them a good hiding. Mothers came to my mother to complain bitterly about this monster of a child. I could tell many stories of my misdeeds.

THE SHOEMAKER'S APPRENTICE

Now the situation became serious. My parents decided I was a good-for-nothing. I would never be a good student. I was in the first grade of the high school, and at the bottom of my class. So my father said to my mother, "Let him become a shoemaker." They decided to send me to a shoemaker as an apprentice. I was very happy at this decision. Not to go to school any more! Not to be compelled to learn Latin and mathematics. It sounded like a release from the tortures of hell. Not to be looked upon as if I were a dumbbell. Not to stay a second year in the class! Wasn't it much better to become a shoemaker?

One day I was taken to the shoemaker, Mueller, and articled to him as an apprentice. The master was a kind and witty man.

This life was to my taste. To loaf around, to listen to the talks of the grownups, to have no school, no coaching, no lessons; it seemed to me like life in a fairy tale. My first disappointment was the so-called "second breakfast" at which each person received a liqueur glass of schnapps and a piece of black bread. I could not stand the schnapps, and the bread was hard and tasted bitter. I hurried home to ask for bread and butter. Mother was not in the kitchen, but I saw a row of warm, fragrant loaves of white bread on the table. Mother had baked them. This was an art of which she was rightly proud. I seized one of the loaves, took it back to my master, and said, "With greetings from my mother! Half of this loaf is for you, half for me." The master enjoyed it very much and I overcame my first disappointment— and then came another.

There were three of us apprentices at Mueller's. We ran errands and were supposed to take turns in bringing repaired shoes to their owners. I was told that the apprentice who did this work received a few pennies as a tip. I greedily awaited my turn, but imagine my chagrin when they ignored me and sent another apprentice to deliver the new shoes. The other boy would get the tip I had anticipated receiving. I felt the injustice bitterly and ran away. I told my mother firmly that a hundred wild horses would not drag me back to the shoemaker.

That was the only time I ever received a good hiding from my father. My mother, whose pet child I was in

spite of my bad behavior, stopped the hiding. I promised to improve at school. I had to repeat the class I had
left. At the end of the school year my marks were above
average.

My later school years were negotiated with ease. At
the end of three years I had become one of the best
pupils. I was fond of my parents, but was not attached
to them. I had many playmates and was decidedly extro-
verted.

MY FAMILY

Now is the time to speak about my family. My father
was a slim, well-built man whose fundamental charac-
teristics were kindness, honesty, and a longing for
knowledge. He liked jokes, was merry, good-hearted,
and benevolent. His pride was that he had acted all his
life according to the proprieties and the law. Thoroughly honest himself, he misplaced confidence in
others, and many times he was cheated by his partners
and friends. Shortly before his death he said to me, "I
can't leave you money but I can leave you something
that is more than money, my honest name. I have never
trespassed. I am proud that I have never been called to
court either as a plaintiff or as a defendant." When he
married my mother he was an illiterate man. He was an
orthodox Jew. My mother made him free from all
prejudices, and Father tried to acquire knowledge in
every way possible. His favorite books were history
books, and many times he remarked what a wonderful
book Graetz's *History of the Jews* was. Later he became
a freethinker and a strongly ethical individual. I may

have inherited from him much of the good in my temperament, my benevolence, and my contempt for money. Mother called him a spendthrift.

Later I learned that my mother was his second wife. His first marriage was unhappy. He was all the fonder, therefore, of my mother who, incidentally, was a charming and pretty woman.

His emancipation advanced speedily. He read the best modern books with Mother, dropped his old ways, and even outstripped her, for he had a good literary taste, something which she lacked. His morals were strict, his sense of honor was beyond reproach, but he was as credulous as a child. His kindliness was such that we children never had a harsh word from him.

My mother had one peculiar quality. She detested servants, without exception, declaring that they were our salaried enemies. She was somewhat miserly, and this had its effect upon the domestics. The result was that our servants seldom stayed long.

Mother was in one respect like father; she came from a plain, narrowly-educated family, and early in life she hungered for knowledge. As a girl she had to hide in the garret to read Schiller because it was forbidden to read anything except Holy Scriptures. She liked philosophical books. Indeed, she enjoyed any book. Once when I was walking with her, a locksmith, laden with chains, passed by. "You see," she said, "they are using chains to bar the harbor. Now the fugitive is trapped."

"What do you mean?" I queried.

"Oh . . . I'm sorry," she apologized, "my mind is in the novel I've been reading." She could not tolerate life without a book. In her spare time she sat in a corner where she simultaneously knitted socks and read. Her educational method was marvelous. Without having read anything on the subject, she found the right way. When I was naughty, she never threatened that God would punish me. Religion was not mentioned but she always spoke of the high values of ethics. Once I asked my mother, "Are there devils?"

"Wicked people are devils," she answered. "Do right, and you will have nothing to fear." Many times she preached to me, "Money doesn't count in life. You can lose it. But no one can deprive you of your knowledge." I was seventy years old when through the *Anschluss* I lost my home, my savings, my medical and musical instruments, my music, part of my library, but I could take this knowledge with me to London and create a new existence. As far as money was concerned, I was always the loser. I have lost my savings five times. But I never felt these losses deeply.

I remember an episode from a later period of my boyhood. Father had secured a position abroad and regularly sent a small sum home. Thus, thanks to the economy of my mother, we could live modestly without fear of starvation.

Every child is a little spy. I got to know that my father had an affair abroad with his landlady. Father came home for a holiday. He knew that my mother was aware of his adventure. He expected reproaches, but nothing happened. Then Mother, while cleaning his trunk, found a present he had purchased for his "other woman." She upbraided him, not because he had had an affair, but because of the expense. She knew that father loved only her. Even as an old woman she was still receiving love letters from him. Reading these letters she would smile happily and say, "The old fool."

Although she was economical, she was a spendthrift on education. My sister, a gifted pianist, had the best and most expensive teachers. I was advised to take piano lessons from my sister and Mother gave me two *kreutzers* for each lesson, otherwise I would never have learned to play. How thankful I am to my mother for this little premium! From the pedagogical aspect it was superior to coercion. I wanted to learn to skate. Mother gave me the tuition money and she was equally generous when I wanted to learn to swim. My sister and her friends spoke French. "Learn French," said my mother, "then you will understand what the girls are gossiping about."

I was always acutely hungry. I was never forced to eat, and for that I am grateful to Mother. I have never lost my appetite; on the other hand, I never became gluttonous.

Mother's simple philosophical formulas were the guides of my life. "Never repent having to renounce pleasure," she once said. Then she told me the story of a man who had a ticket for a pleasure trip by boat, but was prevented by urgent business from taking the trip. The boat sank and many persons drowned.

Mother was a wonderful woman. I dedicated my best book, *A Primer for Mothers,* to her.

She instinctively recognized what I learned after many years of psychiatric experience; the value of training by love. This kind of education automatically reduces hatred. It is a mistake to introduce hatred into school education as was done for patriotic reasons in France after World War I. French children were taught "not to forget." To be able to forget and to forgive is a prerogative of noble souls. We see how often the punishment children receive from parents is not forgotten or forgiven. The task of the psychiatrist is to reduce the power of inner hatreds and aggressions. He must show the individual who cannot forgive his parents how often the parents themselves are unhappy people who project their personal woes into their children. I often quote the following touching scene from Dostoyevsky's life. A stranger on the street slapped his face. The poet looked up to him with deep sympathy and said, "How unhappy you must be if you can hit a stranger."

Training through love breeds love. The Swiss poet Herman Hesse[1] recognizes it when in his Indian poem, *Sidhartha,* he writes the following dialogue: "Tell me my dear, you do not educate your son? You do not force him, do not hit him, do not punish him?"

"No, I do none of these things."

"I knew it. You do not force him, do not hit him, do not command him, because you know that Soft is stronger than Hard, Water stronger than Rock, Love stronger than Force. But do you not bind him with the tie of your love? Do you not shame him daily and make it hard for him with all your goodness and patience?"

What is the most important duty of parents? To make their child apt for life, happy and independent. My parents were equal to the task. I look back upon my long life—I am now seventy-two years old—and ask myself,

---

[1] He was awarded the Nobel Prize for literature in 1949.—*The Editor.*

"If you were born again, what sort of life would you choose?" I answer, "I should gladly repeat the same life with its sufferings and joys, its disappointments and successes." I should not wish for a different life, because, taking everything into account, I have always been a happy person. For this reason I believe that I have the right to handle the problems of education, and to advise parents. In doing this I am drawing upon my forty years of experience as a psychotherapist whose task has been to correct the results of faulty education.

I have learned through experience that most neurotics are victims of faulty education and unhappy environment. Many of my patients were the offspring of unhappily married parents. The well-known saying, "The criminal is the crime of the state," can be paralleled by, "The neurotic is the crime of the family."

The ethical influence of my parents was firmly planted in me. But it was ethics without religion. We were, with the exception of my sister, freethinkers. Looking back at her life I understand that she was an obsessional parapath.[2] She shunned the cemetery, and, in contrast to the rest of the family, she was fanatically religious. She had a tattered prayer book and three times a day she would go into a corner of the room to say her prayers. She wanted me to become religious, and she paid me two *kreutzers* for every prayer I said. This sum supplemented the small income I received for *taking* piano lessons and the prodigious fee of two *gulden* which I was paid for tutoring a pupil in his school

---

[2] Notice that Stekel uses the term "parapath" which he proposed for "neurotic."—*The Editor.*

subjects. With the first *gulden* I earned, I bought a silver thimble for my mother.

Then came a radical change in my general outlook on life. I was fed up with the Red Indian stories, and started the *Tales of Hoffman* (now out of fashion). There was always the story of the boy who was in grave danger of becoming a criminal, and who, after divers adventures and misfortunes, turned out to be a successful and honest gentleman. There was a second-hand bookshop where for a penny I could exchange one little book for another. I used my money to get these books.

Now came another turning-point in my life. A cousin who was my age often came to visit me. One day he began to talk to me about bad boys who visit houses of ill-fame. We excelled in virtue, and together ran down these corrupt boys. But we repeated the same talk every day, and after a fortnight we went together to the house in question. When I returned home, I experienced my first sleepless night. I was then fourteen years old.

This episode had unexpected consequences. Before this expedition I was a stargazer, a daydreamer, a mooncalf, and I could not pay much attention to the teachers. Now I rose to the top of the class and became a teacher of boys who had been at the top in the lower grades. I became an idealist; the period of wildness was finished forever. It was then that I wrote my first poem. I longed for an ideal love with a girl, a love separated from the world of sex. Ideal love and gratification from a prostitute became opposite poles. I chummed with a youth who had the same ambition—to become a great poet. We exchanged good books, reveled in the beauties of nature, and read our poems to each other.

MUSIC

My financial situation was much improved. I earned
some money and was able to afford my own expenses.
Father was abroad, my sister was employed as a governess in Vienna. My brother worked as a clerk away
from home. However, we had to be cautious on mone-
tary matters.

Our lodging was too big for just Mother and me, so
my mother advertised in the newspaper for a roomer.
An old Czech school teacher with his son, a thorough
scalawag, applied. The son had been expelled from
school in Prague. His father, a Mr. Peck, was not well
off, and so he bargained with my mother. Finally it
was agreed that Mr. Peck would pay six *shillings* a
month, and in addition Mr. Peck would continue my
piano lessons. Mr. Peck could play some dances on the
piano. His school salary was meager. By playing the
piano and the violin at the nearby inn he earned the
major part of his income. He asked me to play something and I responded with the not overly-difficult
"Sonata in G Minor" by Beethoven. Mr. Peck was
astonished. He rushed to my mother. "The boy plays the
piano better than I do!" Mother was pleased. She had
one of her typically glorious ideas: "Everything the
boy learns will be of advantage in his future years." She
bought a cheap violin, and Mr. Peck started to teach
me. I was rough on the poor man because I had no
sense of pitch. The noise I made on the fiddle was
nerve-wracking. But I made rapid progress. Subsequently, as a medical student, I played the violin in an
amateur orchestra; later I learned to play the viola and

participated in a string quartet. I am grateful to my mother for the many pleasurable hours my training in music has afforded me.

At the piano I first attempted the most difficult pieces, and neglected the bass. "You are climbing the rungs of the ladder too quickly." It did not matter; I learned to improvise and this ability helped me over many hours which otherwise would have been arduous. I regret that I did not learn harmony and counterpoint, but once I began improvising on the piano, my inventive power seemed inexhaustible. I learned everything by myself. Had I possessed a trustworthy sense of pitch, I would have become a musician. I believe that the artistic gift is not one-sided. A creative mind can express itself in any branch of art. I also tried to draw, but I could go no further than the infantile beginnings. My son, by the way, is a distinguished composer and has a perfect sense of pitch; my daughter is an able painter.

THE HIGH SCHOOL

In the small town of Czernowitz there was only a German high school and a German university. The inhabitants of the town were of four nationalities: Rumanian, Polish, Ukrainian, and German. German was the colloquial language. Jews were considered as Germans, and we Jews felt that we were Germans. It never occurred to me that I was not a German. The word "anti-Semitism" was unknown in Czernowitz. In our class the students felt like brothers; the spirit of solidarity was so strong that it was impossible for the teachers to find a telltale if one of us misbehaved. There were many gifted boys of diverse nationalities. We founded a poetry club, met every Saturday night, and even arranged a poetry writing competition. The German teacher was the judge. Once I received the first prize for lyric and epic verses.

At school we were up to all kinds of pranks; we got together to drink beer and to joke and sing. We often frolicked until late at night. Then, on the following morning, Mother would come to breakfast with her head wrapped in a woolen scarf and complain of migraine. She would pretend that she had been unable to sleep until she heard me arrive. She gave me an unctuous sermon about the dangers of vice. I would reply with a laconical display of erudition: "Mother, two thousand years ago Socrates delivered the same lecture." Once Mother changed the sermon, "You must understand me, I am not narrow-minded, but if an artist sees how the growing work of art is going to seed, he must try to prevent it from deteriorating completely."

My fellow students were going to dancing school, but Mother refused to permit me to join them. I pretended that I had to visit a student to help him prepare for the next day's school work. But I headed directly for the dancing school where I quickly became a good dancer. Prior to taking dancing lessons I often played at the dancing school when my sister, her friends, and other young people held impromptu dances.

The bond among the students in my class was so strong that the principal tried to keep us in check by assigning the strictest master to us. This schoolmaster endured much, but after six months he gave up. If we liked a teacher, we could be extremely well-mannered. There was, for example, Professor F., in the chair of mathematics. The students were fond of him because he was just and witty. Five minutes before he appeared in the classroom, we were quietly seated at our desks with our work well-prepared. F. would stroke his beard and smile —he was at a loss to understand our bad reputation. We had a wonderful time with him. We loved especially the Tyrolian teacher, Passler, who taught German and history. Each of his lectures was splendidly prepared, each address a remarkable experience—we looked forward to every lesson we had with him. These two examples prove that the behavior of pupils depends, in a large measure, upon the teachers. Our Latin and Greek teacher, whom we had from the first to the eighth class, was esteemed because he was just and human; he never complained about our conduct. However, let us draw the veil over the other schoolmasters—the dry perfectionists to whom historical dates were more important than real wisdom and to whom a wrong Greek aorist was sufficient cause to compel a pupil to repeat an entire year's work and thus burden a family with doubt and embarrassment. I do not exaggerate when I say that the fate of humanity lies in the hands of teachers. I consider it to be the foremost duty of the state to take care of its teachers to the extent that they do not become embittered, that they maintain their joy of life and share it with their pupils. It is a duty of both the family and the school to bring up happy and independent people. It is regrettable that governments which have huge sums for armaments and wars are so miserly in budgeting their educational programs. In my opinion, education should be the most respected and rewarded item in the budgets of the governments of the world.

Fifty years after our class matriculated, we had a re-union. More than twenty of us gathered together for this celebration. What an assembly of old ghosts we were! The American author, Washington Irving, would have regarded his amusing and enlightening Rip van Winkle as a prosaic fellow, indeed, had he seen us. We tried futilely to rekindle the fire of our former enthusiasm. We found that we were indifferent to each other. We were strangers who tried to behave as though we were friends. Fifty years before we had vanished from each other's lives. Now we were back. But physical proximity could not restore our warmth. The reunion was a dismal failure!

FIRST LOVE

Which of our emotions is lasting? I mentioned that I wrote poems, mostly about nature, and some humorous ones. Then came the event that made me feel like a true poet. As I was walking along the usual promenade, an extremely pretty girl, Bertha, looked at me. It came like a lightning flash—love at first sight. I ran to my friends and declared, "I am very happy because I am unhappily in love." Now a regular stream of poems flowed. I made eyes at Bertha on every occasion, usually from a distance. When she sent me a message telling me not to stare at her, I continued to gaze at her, but from a longer distance. I was happy in the unhappiness that provided the inspiration for new poems. For a long time I could not understand why I loved her at first sight.

Then I noticed that *my mother had the same slanting look and the same eyes.* Love at first sight is a revival of an infantile impression. The first love object reappears in a different disguise. The crystallization of such an ideal usually originates in early childhood; the ideal in reality represents the past projected into the future. I kept my ideal apart from my carnal experiences.

BETWEEN MATERIALISM AND IDEALISM

The mixture of idealism and materialism was evident at this period of my life. While I had dreams of becoming a great poet, I tried to build my physical strength by exercise and continence. I spent all available free time at the gymnasium or on long hikes with my friends. I also set some of my own poems to music. At first, my friends laughed at my efforts. Later I was more clever and disguised my compositions as songs by Schubert—then the poems were enthusiastically applauded. Years later I heard one of my songs in a students' fraternity; it had found its way to the public. Many students learned my songs, and the songs were passed on from person to person. They were accepted only when they were believed to be compositions by Schubert or Schumann.

Years passed. School was like play for me; in the afternoon I gave lessons, but I had enough time for reading and music. However, the day I left high school (*Gymnasium*) was one of the happiest of my life. The freedom which followed the restrictions of the school made me feel as though I were drunk with champagne. We, the happy ones, the higher beings, strutted back and forth along the promenade, canes in our hands, the latter a violation of one of the school's strictest regulations. I longed to study the German language and the history of mankind, but the prospects of so doing were poor. Besides, I was eager to see Vienna. The University of Czernowitz had no medical faculty. The study of medicine offered a good reason for me to go to Vienna.

At the final examination everybody was asked to state what he was going to study. I answered, "German and history." The good old principal, Wolf, called out, "You ought to become a journalist." I had not thought of this career before, but I knew that since I had a definite talent in this direction, I could fall back upon it in an emergency.

Then came a joyful vacation time. The governor of the county, Baron W., invited me to stay with him on his estate. I had tutored his son, a fellow student, successfully and now I was to coach another son in Latin.

At Baron W.'s I learned about the lives of aristocrats from many angles. There was always an abundance of guests, and they did not think that the baron would have invited a Jew. Thus I had the opportunity to listen to many frank and unrestrained anti-Semitic talks. I was astounded. I had not realized that the Jew played such a part in the discussions of Gentiles. I felt sorry for these guests. Even then I realized that by blaming the Jew for all of their own failings and by projecting their own guilt feelings upon him, they were tragically depriving themselves of the opportunity for a radical improvement and spiritual progress.

Chapter Two

UNIVERSITY DAYS

★

Now it was time to go to Vienna. I was eager for life in a big city with its limitless possibilities. My savings would provide for only one month's expenses. I therefore decided to earn my living as a tutor.

On the morning after my arrival, I went to the central district of Vienna to peruse the "ads" which a popular newspaper displayed. There was a crowd of students. Each would-be tutor noted the addresses of prospective employers, and then hurried off to get work. I found a position in the home of a *parvenu,* a baker. The contrast with the aristocratic milieu of the baron was too much for me to tolerate. I was accustomed to a peaceful home, and the atmosphere of these newly-rich people was horrid. Let us not go into details of my experiences in this house.

I became inured to Viennese life. I studied art in the museums, hired a cheap upright piano on which I practiced whenever possible. Once a week I played second violin in an amateur orchestra. Despite my many extra-curricular activities, I was a successful student and

55

passed my examinations with excellent marks. During vacation, I returned home. At a party in my home town I met my former great love, Bertha, to whom I had dedicated countless poems. I asked her to dance—she was in my arms. No doubt she wanted to start a flirtation. Years ago such a situation would have brought heights of ecstasy. Now it was she who was making advances, and I was cold to her. Other girls interested me much more, but I was fearful of any lasting attachment. Short episodes suited me better.

In Vienna, I made the acquaintance of a cultured family whose standard of living was markedly different from that of the baker—fine music, literature, profound conversation. And once a week a little literary circle met with these stimulating people. At this home I was introduced to Mrs. R., a widow, who earned her livelihood by taking students as boarders. She invited me to come to her home as often as convenient for me, and to stay for dinner. She had a piano which we both enjoyed playing. I met many interesting people in her home; and, as she lived near my own lodgings, I availed myself of every opportunity to visit her.

My time was fully occupied. I was a busy student and did not miss any lectures. Nor did I neglect my physical well-being—twice a week I went to the academic gymnasium; afterward, my companions and I went to a restaurant where a private dining room was at our disposal, and here we spent many happy hours in song. At that time I was the conductor of a singing society, many members of which were my close friends. One evening a week I played in the orchestra and on still another evening I played in a string quartet.

My plan to earn my living by giving lessons was realized. My expenses were small, and were kept within the bounds of my income. I ate my lunch at a popular-priced restaurant; at night I ate apples and bread and butter; and for breakfast I brewed tea. To get to the places where I gave lessons, I had to use the streetcar which at that time was horse-drawn. Sometimes, it took a half-hour or more to reach my destination, and I employed that time in reading scientific books.

During those years I made considerable progress at the piano and soon played almost all the sonatas of Mozart and Beethoven. I enjoyed my own compositions, and continued to compose songs. I did not frequent coffee-houses as was customary among the students of Vienna, and seldom did I go to the opera. When, on rare occasions, I attended a theatre, I usually had to stand in the queue for four or five hours to get a good "standing" place. But I had a wonderful time during these student days.

MILITARY SERVICE

Military service for medical students was divided into two periods. For half of the year we served as ordinary soldiers, the other half, as physicians. I decided to spend my service time in Czernowitz. This half-year of military service was the most disagreeable period of my life. I had always been a pacifist. Moreover, I was unaccustomed to severe discipline; I found the "soldier play" ridiculous and contrary to humanity. With this attitude toward the military service I had the misfortune to be under a sergeant who had a notorious reputation for cruelty and severity. Only the year before, a colleague of mine had killed himself because he was unable to endure the harshness of this sergeant. I was an excellent soldier, and able to endure the gruelling, exhausting demands of a soldier's life.

I remember one field drill on a very hot summer day. I was carrying a heavy pack, and had been marching for miles. At this time I was head of an ambulance. Right and left, soldiers were collapsing from sunstroke and fatigue. I shall never forget that terrible day, filled with torment and cruelty, all in the guise of military training; no part of it contributing to efficiency in war, or to the service of humanity, or to the future of mankind.

The day I left the army with the rank of corporal was one of the happiest days of my life. I felt free once more —no longer at the beck and call of commonplace people. Again, I was master of my time. I felt as though I could start a new life. In a sense, I felt I had been reborn.

It seems paradoxical, therefore, that at this time I permitted my family to persuade me to accept a military scholarship, entailing the obligation to remain in military service for six years as an army doctor. I received a monthly allowance, in addition to which all the expenses of examinations and post-graduate courses were paid for by the State.

It became increasingly difficult to combine this job with my own studies. But I was encouraged by the words of Goldhaber, the army surgeon who gave a course in first aid to the military medical students. At the end of the course he said, "My young colleagues, one word before we part. We military surgeons are often the only ones who can defend the poor man from the ranks against chicanery and injustice."

I consoled myself with Goldhaber's injunction, for I felt it was my duty to fight for the rights of man, if only in my own limited sphere.

My position was now much improved. I could make use of my afternoons in the clinic to examine the new cases before the assistant made his diagnoses. During the vacations I worked in the skillfully administered, well-equipped hospital at Czernowitz. I assisted at operations, and was continually striving to increase my medical knowledge.

ACUTE ILLNESS

During my student days I was in perfect health. As a youngster I had gone through almost all the common diseases of childhood, including diphtheria and small-pox. Now, during my service at the hospital in Czerno-witz, I was stricken by sudden headaches and by transient depressions. "You are overworked," I told myself. "You need a rest." I decided to travel through the Carpathians and thus to gratify an old desire. I packed my knapsack and began hiking. Whenever possible I spent the nights with relatives or friends in order to save money.

In a beautiful valley I had my first nightmare: *I am in a dark room. A monster, half bear and half ape, black, with glowing eyes, comes near to my bed and tries to choke me. Then this monster speaks, "You must die." I try to fight it off, and I awake shouting.*[1]

---

[1] Stekel did not recognize at that time that this dream represented a warning of an impending danger. Dreams of this type frequently precede infectious diseases. They are dreamt in subfebrile conditions.— *The Editor.*

After a swim in the river, I would pick up my knapsack and start off again. I must mention that during this time I bathed twice a day in different rivers and ponds and whenever possible I took a long swim. So I moved on from place to place, climbing high mountains, crossing rivers and valleys—I had never even dreamed of such magnificent scenery. Night after night I shivered slightly, but thought this of little importance.

I came to a charming village. I had two letters of introduction—one to a priest and one to a doctor in this community. I first visited the priest. He lived in a pretty house surrounded by lime trees. Many flowers bloomed in the foreground. The door was wide open and I walked in. A big room and a piano! Like a man dying of thirst I rushed to the instrument. I improvised, deeply immersed in my fantasies. After perhaps a half-hour I stopped. To my astonishment there were applause and cries of *Bravo!* I looked around and saw about ten people. I had not heard them enter. On the street a little crowd had gathered to listen. I was invited to stay at the house, but I refused this offer and excused myself as I wanted to see the doctor about my nocturnal shivering.

The doctor was pleased to see me. In these isolated villages any visitor was a welcome variation. In any house I invariably looked for the library, for then I knew what kind of people the owners were. Such observations afforded quick information. The doctor said to me, "You are considering my library? I haven't read these books for many years. I only read Wieland now. I am reading him for the third time from cover to cover."

I was astonished. The poet, Wieland, once a rival of Goethe, had never particularly impressed me. The doctor was a man who had a one-track mind about literature. Later I met many men who read "only" Shakespeare or Goethe or Voltaire—and, perhaps, the Bible. *Chacun à son goût.*

I asked the doctor's opinion about my night shivers. He took my temperature. It was above normal, but he thought this resulted from unusual bodily exertion. So I resumed my journey at a slower pace. After a week I came to the last place of my pilgrimage and I was joyously received by friends who arranged a gay dinner. Even the older gentlemen at the party sang like young students. (How different from the sour and bemused faces at the fiftieth anniversary of the class matriculation!) The feasting and gayety continued until after midnight, but to my surprise I could eat scarcely anything because of a peculiar distaste for food.

On the next day I returned home. My father was aghast when he saw me. I had become terribly thin, and my cheeks were flushed. He called in our family physician who said I was suffering from ambulatory typhoid. The entire time I was walking, climbing, swimming, I had been seriously ill.

The convalescence made slow progress. I had lost forty pounds, and was so weak I could scarcely walk. The appetite after an attack of typhoid is wonderful. Can it be true that typhoid means the cleansing of the body? *Sterilisatio magna?* I went as a boarder to a Mrs. E., the mother of the aforementioned artistic violin player in our string quartet. She felt sorry for me and gave me the biggest helpings imaginable. Between meals I had to run to the grocer where I bought cheap rolls and sausages which I devoured hungrily and with the keenest relish. After two months I had regained my weight and vigor.

THE PACIFIST MOVEMENT

Now came a new phase. My brother, who had a considerable journalistic talent, a wonderful style, and a pen for satire, was now editor of a journal in Czernowitz. He had written an enthusiastic review of a book by Baroness Suttner, *Lay Down Arms*. In this way he got in touch with her. Later he sent me the book. I wrote the Baroness a letter, and proposed to be the founder of a University Pacifists' Club. She was enraptured with the idea, and invited me to a meeting at Prince Wrede's. I was embarrassed. What kind of formalities would there be? Evening clothes?—What was the correct way to address him?

I went to the Prince's home in my best clothes. He was a kind old gentleman who lived in a half-ruined palace. He offered his premises for our club. On that occasion were present the Baroness Suttner and the famous psychiatrist, Krafft-Ebing, who was an ardent pacifist. I explained the plan of the club, and Krafft-Ebing promised his help. Baroness Suttner invited me to a supper "at the Archduke Karl's." This appeared really embarrassing—after the prince an "archduke"! I had no dress suit, and was ill-informed about the necessary ceremony. Baroness Suttner gave me the address, in the central district of Vienna. Curious, I went to the place in order to inspect the Archduke's palace. What a disappointment when I realized that I had been invited to supper at the "Hotel Archduke Karl."

We had a very nice evening, and talked about the details of the propaganda. The Baroness was one of the most charming women I have ever met; she may have been five to eight years older than her husband. He died many years earlier than she. An impoverished countess of the Kinsky family, the Baroness had become a governess in the castle of the Suttner's; the young son Gundaker fell in love with her and they eloped to the Caucasus. When their means were exhausted they both tried to earn a living by writing. She was more successful than her husband, who published some mediocre novels. Her book, *Lay Down Arms,* and a second one, *The Machine Age,* are worth reading even today. This noble-hearted woman did not live to witness the Great War and its atrocities, and I am happy that during her long life she saw many of the brighter periods of human dignity and stability.

I had many friends of various nationalities. Among them was the leader of the anti-Semitic group in the University, a Mr. S. One day I was sitting on a bench at the hospital, and he addressed me. I was astonished and said, "What's come over you? You talk to a Jew?" S. answered, "Last Sunday they thought I was a Jew. I was treated so roughly that my eyes were opened on this question. All my life I will fight against anti-Semitism." He kept his word.

We pacifists posted bills inviting others to join the club, and we were able to enroll over fifty members. We had cozy meetings, and dreamed of times when there would be no war. In this club there were representatives of all nationalities. Everyone wanted me to be the chairman. I recommended another student for president, and the man I named was elected. Spiritually, however, I was the leader.

In this year there was a large international meeting of pacifists at Berne, and pacifist members of various parliaments came together for the first time. Baroness Suttner wanted me to attend this meeting as the representative of the University Pacifist Club and to make the attempt to establish an International Pacifist Union of Students. She procured the money for my journey. My sister, who at that time spoke French and English fluently, was willing to accompany me on the trip.

We made the journey together, and we always shared the same room. In one hotel I booked myself "Stekel and *Sister*" and the next morning we found in the book the remark, "Is the dye fast?" We both laughed.

After the profound and vivid impression of Salzburg and Innsbruck, we came to Munich and I visited the famous "Hofbrauhaus" and enjoyed the justly-famed Bavarian beer. I could not understand why my sister should find this beer disgusting. A pleasure not shared by your companion is only half a pleasure.

FRENCH

We all spoke only French at all times in order to prepare discussions at the meeting. How did I learn this beautiful language? I may interpolate this characteristic episode: Through a cousin I obtained a well-paid job as a tutor to the son of a rich manufacturer whom I was to prepare for his examination in mathematics. This examination was called "The Intelligence Examination," and carried the privilege of reducing military service from three years to one. I was always an exceptionally good teacher and my pupil made rapid progress. One day he said to me, "I am sure I'll pass in mathematics, but I'm weak in French. Could you teach me French?"

I had no (teaching) knowledge of French, but the temptation was overwhelming. It was not a question of French conversation; you had only to translate some passages from German into French and conversely. I agreed to do so, but with the condition that we start from the first paragraph of the grammar. I purchased a grammar which was recommended for this examination, studied the first part, and thus, well-prepared, I repeated this lesson with my pupil until he had a perfect knowledge of it. He was satisfied with my procedure; later he received the first prize in French at his examination.

Then I used my freshly acquired knowledge to read the best French books and to translate French poems. I always used a dictionary. A friend of mine who was ten years my senior and spoke several languages observed me browsing in the dictionary, and said, "You are wasting your time. You ought to read books without a dictionary, and little by little you will understand the sense of the words. You must learn a language like a child, by listening to it, or by reading it."

I followed this advice and passed on to Rousseau's
Confessions, one of the most impressive books I have
ever read. To tell the truth about your own life—this
was a new thought! I think it was then that the intention
of writing my own confessions was born. From then on
I read the best French books. In Zola, I found a realistic
description of sex life and a new way of writing novels.
As a psychoanalyst one can easily recognize that most
novels conceal true life; what is hidden behind the cur-
tain of the plot is often more important than what is
exposed in the book. Freud told me once, when we were
walking in the forest of Berchtesgaden, "In my mind, I
always construct novels, using my experiences as a psychoanalyst; my wish is to become a novelist—but not yet;
perhaps in the later years of my life. . . ."

Everyone has had a book, I should say the only book,
that has made the deepest impression on him. I used to
ask my patients what the title was of this "only book."
It gave me an immediate insight into their minds. If
the patient answered *Crime and Punishment,* or *Faust,*
or the *Bible,* or a detective novel, I knew what kind of
person I was dealing with. If the answer was, "no outstanding book," that was equally significant.

My own deepest literary impression was produced by
a novel of the Norwegian, Arne Gaborg, called *Peasant
Students.* I was enraptured by the way this author spoke
about sexual matters. Later I read all his other books.
It is my habit to do this if a writer appeals to me.

I practiced French with my sister; she corrected my
mistakes and I was soon well enough prepared to follow
the discussions.

THE PACIFIST CONGRESS

We reached Berne. In order to save money I carried our two trunks myself. A strange man came up to me and offered to carry one of them. I refused. He was angry. "Do you take me for a thief? I only offered to help you because I see that they are too heavy for you." This was my introduction to Switzerland and the kindness of the people of this country.

We came to the house whose address Baroness Suttner had given me. I had been given a letter of introduction to the hostess, but I did not present it. I obtained the address of my lodgings, and also of a place where I could get very good but inexpensive meals.

I cannot describe the wonderful atmosphere of our meetings. We were like a big family, brothers and sisters; among us were a number of famous men, as well as many well-known members of parliament. I was introduced to various people by Baroness Suttner, and finally to an Italian member of parliament, Marquis Pandolfi. These private meetings prior to the general discussions were a new world for me. No regard was paid to rank, title, or race, and there were no formalities. I, as a poor student, was treated in the same way as Marquis Pandolfi. After the third day of our meetings, an impromptu dance was arranged. I played the piano first, and was followed by Baroness Suttner, and later by an old Italian general who had become a pacifist, after much personal experience with the cruelties of war. The President of Switzerland danced with the porter's wife, the porter with the Baroness, and I with all and sundry.

We were invited by the Government to a trip on Lake Lucerne. I shared the compartment with the President of Switzerland; we had a nice talk, and I thought: "This is a free country. It looks like a paradise. No difference is made between classes, or degrees of wealth." I decided then to spend my life in Switzerland. Such were my thoughts of this nation; but my actual path led elsewhere.

Some of the speeches were wonderful. There was the speech of the Italian general, which ended as follows: "At the dusk of my life I can see the dawn of a new time. In my youth everybody spoke of war and the wicked neighbors. Now we discuss the fraternity of different nations, eternal peace. I feel as though the gates of heaven have been opened."

I am sorry to say that interspersed among the different prominent personages were also many ordinary cranks. At times I had the feeling that the fanatics, paranoiacs, and fools of the whole world had made a rendezvous in Berne. How greatly the idea of eternal peace troubled these people! Often I would be buttonholed in a corner by a man who gave me a booklet and started a long harangue to the effect that only the general adoption of *Volapük* (a "universal language," in fashion before Esperanto) could solve the problem of peace. Another held forth on plans for the United States of the World. A third interceded for a universal currency. These were the fanatics with fixed ideas. Then came the real paranoiacs, the inventors, the anarchists, the reformers—it was a veritable Tower of Babel. Each of these people had come to the Congress in order to find a rostrum from which he could expound his ideas and exhibit his oratory.

Even more inferior as harbingers of peace were the politicians, representatives of suppressed nations, of different parties and national minorities who disturbed the unanimity of the proceedings. Baroness Suttner was desperate, and she did everything possible to exclude politics from the discussions. Often she was imposed upon, disappointed, and made the victim of disagreeable clashes. Fanatics among the politicians tried to further their own brands of enthusiasm, using the pacifist movement as their sounding board.

I used the presence of students of different nationalities as a means of advancing my idea for an International League of Academic Pacifists. I was fortunate enough to get the support of six representatives of different nationalities; I did not succeed in enlisting the Rumanians, the largest group of students, possibly numbering a dozen, who were enthusiastic only about their own protestations against the treatment of Rumanians in Hungary. I, as a young man of twenty-two, made my first public speech. I spoke in German as a representative of the Academic Youth of Vienna. This speech was translated into French and English.

At the congress a pleasant Frenchman often engaged me in conversation, and one day he presented me with a box of expensive sweets. I was at a loss to understand this. He took my address and later, in Vienna, I received a letter from him. He was a member of a group of men who called themselves the Friends of Tuesday Evenings. He sent me a booklet with a description of the evenings and a collection of his poems which contained many lines about friendship and love. At the end of the letter was the phrase, "All the services you render to our members will be rendered by them to you." Now I understood, it was an international group of homosexuals; they had members throughout the world. I did not answer this letter.

THE DUEL

I returned home to study for the final examinations, and in defiance of my convictions I became involved in a quarrel which led to a duel. I was always amazed that the majority of Germans set themselves above defenseless Jews, especially above the weak Jews who appeared to be the most attractive targets for their jokes and hoaxes. I personally never had to suffer from such abuse. I was strong, and the bullies among the Germans avoided me. At the University there was a Jewish fraternity whose members were excellent fencers; and after the Germans suffered a long succession of defeats they decided that it was beneath the dignity of a German to fight with a Jew. I abhorred the duel as a barbarous custom, and did not believe there would ever be any possibility of engaging in one myself.

One day, in the pathology auditorium a burly German was tormenting a little crippled Jew, a very diligent and good-hearted, but weak lad. Sitting behind him, the German kept on tapping the back of his head with a pencil. At moments like these I cannot hide my feelings. "Aren't you ashamed, you coward, to tease such a weakling?" I asked. "Why don't you try the same game on me?"

He was at a loss for words to answer me. He was an officer in the reserve and had to challenge me to a duel or else he would lose his commission. I, too, had to accept the challenge or else I would forfeit my military scholarship. He sent me his second with the challenge, and a friend of mine, a Christian, became my second. We arranged a duel with swords. I had to learn to fence. I received my training in a fraternity where I had heard one of my songs (they did not know that I was the composer). Soon I made good progress in the art of fencing, and the fellows were proud of me. Perhaps my duelling opponent had heard of my progress, for the entire affair was settled by two letters. He apologized for his behavior to the little Jew, and I apologized for the word "coward."

I must confess that I had dreamed about the duel almost nightly. Was I afraid? I have already mentioned that I was rarely troubled by fear. During the day I was not afraid and felt confident I would maintain the upper hand; but during the night I had exciting dreams tinged by fear. Later as a psychoanalyst I recognized that the duel in a dream is used as an expression of a mental conflict and represents the symbol of unconscious homosexual tendencies.[2]

THE LOSS OF A FRIEND

In a short time, our academic group of pacifists had over one hundred members. We arranged a banquet in

---

2 There is, of course, also a repetitive pattern involved which helps the dreamer to eliminate fear. In this case, repetition turned the duel from a novel to a routine experience.—*The Editor.*

which more than three hundred students took part. Baroness Suttner delivered an impressive speech concluding with the words: "The fact that I can be here among the enthusiastic youths who will defend my ideas in the future makes me happy. This is the crowning of my work. I shall never forget that Stekel set all this in motion. I ask you to drink this glass with three cheers for my young friend, Stekel." There was tumultuous applause. The Baroness embraced and kissed me. I got ready to answer, and had no foreboding that I was going to touch a tender spot in her heart by what I was to say, and that she would shrink away from me. I did not reckon, at that time, with the vanity of even broadminded persons. I explained that it was wrong to believe that single human beings are able to impress the masses and to inaugurate powerful changes in the world. The time must be "prepared," and then the time always finds the person it needs. "If a little bird on the top of a glacier scratches the snow with its claws, and this little clump of snow moves on, it rolls down, becomes larger and larger until it grows to be a powerful avalanche. However, this clump of snow could become an avalanche, roll down and destroy everything in its path, only because of the many strata of snow that lay there, available and prepared for it. Persons are successful if the time is ripe for them, and if the hearts of the masses are prepared for their ideas. Let us hope the avalanche of pacifism will roll down and destroy the fortresses of old-fashioned aggressions, prejudices, and superstitions. If this group has so many members, it is not to my special credit. Let us drink to the health of all the people who are ready to follow our brilliant leader, Baroness Suttner, towards a better future."

Poor woman, she was very disappointed! She really believed the whole pacifist movement was her work alone. She believed in the assured success of this movement. Soon our relations were broken off forever.

Why did I make this speech which antagonized Baroness Suttner? Not until later did I come to understand. I was influenced by an unconscious urge to break away from all social relationship and to isolate myself from the world.

My pupils have often complained of finding me unapproachable, of my never espousing without reserve the cause of even my warmest supporters. Often they have thought that I did not care much for them. Certainly, I have never wanted them to take up the cudgels in my behalf, to be incessantly quoting me and singing my praises. I have not tried to win people to my cause or make recruits. I wanted things to come to me spontaneously—as they usually did, publishers, translators, adherents. The fact was that my world had narrow boundaries so that there was no room in it for anyone except myself and my beloved wife.

The first question I always asked a would-be pupil showed that my motives were fundamentally selfish. It was either "Do you play a musical instrument?" or "Do you play tennis?" Elsewhere in this autobiography I relate the dictum that anyone who wants to win my favor should bring my dog a bone. Silberer, a highly gifted man and one of my most ardent followers, who, like some other psychoanalysts, committed suicide, used always to bring some titbits for my dog, and the creature was glad to welcome him. Others would bring some lumps of sugar. When a lady patient showed the animal these little attentions, I knew that the transference had begun, and that the dog stood for his master.

As I had feared, the time was not yet ripe for the pacifist movement. This movement, founded by intellectuals, never penetrated into the hearts of the masses. Though the philosophy of pacifism is so clear, so logical, one might almost say self-evident, it did not become an overwhelming psychic epidemic. It did not "catch on." If this had happened, would a second World War have been possible? He who knows the psychology of the masses sees that the tendencies suggested by the downward trend (the katagogic tendencies) are stronger than the idealistic ones (the anagogic tendencies.) To lift the masses towards the ideal appears difficult, if not impossible; however, an appeal to the lower instincts, an appeal to hatred, cruelty, to contempt for civilization, will always be accepted. Man is covered with a very thin veneer of culture. Scratch a little—and the beast will appear.

The University Pacifist Club did not last very long. I have learned that you cannot influence the evolution of mankind by idealistic societies. For a short while I was interested in Socialism, but did not become an active socialist. I expected that this movement would improve the social standard of the poor, and that the International League of Working-Men would be powerful enough to prevent any war. The Great War taught me later that the appeal to man's sadistic tendencies, dis-

guised as nationalism, smothers all noble feelings. In
the course of my analytic studies I have found that the
primary attitude of man towards the world is that of
hatred. The antithesis "Friend *vs.* Enemy" originally was
"I *vs.* The World." It is a task of culture to teach mankind how to maintain and to enjoy social relations. The
contrast of "I *vs.* The World" may then turn into "I
together with The World."

Our aboriginal instincts remain ever-active. With the
progress of civilization, the feeling that our environment
is hostile diminishes, the pressure of our inner instincts
creates an enemy within ourselves, an enemy who saps
our vital energies. The greatest danger threatens man
from within. And it is really tragic that in most instances
man does not know this inner enemy. The flight from
the inner enemy may lead to compensatory aggressions.

It is, therefore, the weightiest task of culture to turn
the destructive forces into creative ones. Alas! We are
as yet far from this ideal state. The unhappiness of man
creates an unhappy world; and an unhappy world produces unhappy men: a vicious circle. Looking around
one can see a fateful regression of mankind. Everything
that is beautiful and sublime, the world that love helped
to develop, is in danger of deterioration. And yet we
know that all great works are works of love. Impotence
and frigidity are the ailments of our time. Man seems
to flee from love, and to engage in a useless and senseless struggle between the sexes. We need an education to
love, the only education which can help us overcome
hatred.

ENGAGEMENT

I moved in an interesting literary circle in Vienna and met many poets and writers. Introduced into a new home, I made the acquaintance of my first wife. She was very beautiful, had a nice figure, brown eyes like a deer's and a face like Helène Fourment's in the picture by Rubens, although not so plump. I asked her, "What are you most enthusiastic about? What's your hobby?" I was amazed at her answer: "Ibsen—and chocolate candies."

At this time I had a peculiar gauge for judging my friends. It was a book by an unknown poet, Smital, I believe; the title was *Storm in the Spring*—I do not know how it came into by possession. It contained no action, but it was filled with hidden beauties and lovely descriptions of nature. I loaned this book to girls in whom I was interested. If they commented, "It's a bore," they were finished for me. But Malvina, my first wife, found the book charming. I fell head over heels in love; all my former love affairs had been only passing flirtations, but this seemed to be the right thing. My love was returned.

Children of unhappy marriages often suffer from a fear of marriage. The example of a happy marriage, in which as a child I had the good fortune to share, awakened in me the longing for marriage and a home of my own so early that I could hardly wait for the day of the wedding.

It is worth noting that the very people who suffer from the fear of marriage usually become unhappy in their marriages. They take so long to make a choice, they reflect and hesitate, try and weigh, until at last, tired of doubting, they leap headlong into an ill-considered marriage which apparently justifies their fears. And yet, it is the unpremeditated choice of the mate alone that is responsible for their misfortune. These people have lost their genuine instinct.

I wrote my parents asking for their consent and telling them that I wanted to become engaged to a well-educated girl. One letter after another came back warning me not to do it. My parents maintained that since I was a poor boy, I needed a girl who had money. Mother wrote that one rich man had come to her and proposed that if I married his daughter, he would give me a good dowry and, in addition, support me for two years in Paris to finish my post-graduate training. I had long wanted to go to Paris. This prospect was very tempting; I had been yearning for French life. But my mind was made up. Without the consent of my parents, I spoke to Malvina's father, and we became engaged.

I had to overcome a serious obstacle. I was under obligation to work for six years as a military surgeon. Military surgeons were not allowed to marry unless they deposited with the Army the sum of thirty thousand *gulden*. It was impossible for me to get hold of such a sum, but real love finds a way. We decided to wait the long six years until I obtained my freedom from military duty.

The period of our engagement was one of beauty. For two or three hours each evening we played duets, usually the works of famous classical composers. We read and discussed the same books; we went for long walks in the picturesque surroundings of Vienna; but despite all my emotional entanglements I did not neglect my studies.

Chapter Three

PRACTICING MEDICINE

★

WORK WITH KRAFFT-EBING

EXAMINATIONS were like play to me and they evoked so little concern that even my betrothed did not know their dates. The examination on internal medicine was over. I had always been interested in neurology, and now I had the time to work many hours in the famous clinic of Krafft-Ebing. I supervised two rooms, and achieved fine results—mostly, as I now understand, through transference. Krafft-Ebing liked my work because in two cases I was able to prove my special gift for medicine. One assistant had worked for two years studying the phenomena of the constriction of the visual field. He used the seven primary colors and was able to prove that the visual field in such cases was smaller for some colors than for others. He used them always in the same succession. This examination was made upon hysterical patients. I noticed immediately that he neglected the fact that hysterics are affected by fatigue reaction. I changed the succession of the colors and was able to prove that any subsequent color showed a smaller visual field than the previous one. I communicated my findings to Krafft-Ebing, who was surprised that the clinic had not thought of this fatigue reaction before. I felt very sorry for his assistant, who, by not taking into consideration this important margin of error, lost the fruits of two years' work.

Krafft-Ebing was an outstanding teacher and a leading sexologist, although a less competent neurologist. He took the case histories home, carefully studied the disease he wanted to present on the next day, and then gave one of his famous lectures.

I qualified for graduation, and Krafft-Ebing as Dean gave me the diploma with the words: "I enjoy very much giving this to you." On my way home I met him, and he invited me to stay in his clinic promising me a noted career. What was to be done? Here was the chance to become a professor, a clinician—but I was bound to remain in military service.

THE MILITARY HOSPITAL

First, I worked in a military hospital. The head of this hospital was an excellent specialist for ear, nose, and throat, but he did not care for internal medicine. In a short time he left to me the entire supervision of the internal clinic, reserving for himself only the out-patients. I received good training, and in a short time achieved skill in treating ear, nose, and throat diseases.

However, my foremost thought was about how I could

become free from my military obligations? I had a contract with the Government for six years' service, to be
sure. But nothing was mentioned in this contract that
we had to go through a special examination on the duties
of military service in war. I was well prepared, and anyway, it was a sham examination, for no one ever heard
of anyone failing in it. During the examination of the
candidate preceding me, the idea flashed through my
brain, "You will be the first one to fail in this examination." At the examination I played the part of a dunce
so effectively that I was told I must try again. I simulated
excitement, saying, "Gentlemen, I have hitherto passed
all my examinations with top marks. I am not going to
repeat this one. By my contract I am not obligated to
undergo any further examination." The whole commission was dumbfounded. How were they to treat such
a rebel?

They retired to talk it over and finally I was called in
and told that the commission found me unworthy of
receiving a commission as an army medical officer. I had
to sign a paper agreeing to pay my scholarship money
in installments as soon as I began to earn.

I was free, at last. However, the military authorities
wanted to discipline me, and so I was called for the
second half-year of my military service, to work as a
"cadet" at the same hospital. Most cadets were given
money for outside lodgings, but I had to sleep in the
hospital and to share a room with a cadet from the sani-
tary department. I did not consider all these little annoyances as punishment, because my former superior,
Tschudi, did everything in his power to get me back

again to his clinic. Soon I found myself working under him and having a fine time. Finally, the idea of punishing me was forgotten. On the contrary, I was treated as a man of standing.

According to regulations, an army medical officer should not treat officers or their families outside the hospital; but it was an unwritten law that he do so, and he could even accept gifts, though never money. Tschudi had a large private practice among officers and sometimes I had to assist him and to take care of the after-treatment in families suffering from nose and throat disorders. Tschudi treated me as a good friend. Once in his apartment he said to me, "You were right not to become a medical officer. If I were a private specialist I should be a very rich man. I treat all the officers, even generals and field marshals of Vienna. What's the result? I work like a dog, and earn nothing but my official pay. I get presents, presents, only presents! If my patients were clever enough to send me valuable rings, or jewelled tie-pins. Look around! What do you see? More than thirty different vases. Am I a collector of ceramics? . . . I am not even able to sell them or to give them to someone else, that would be a mortal offense."

He opened a chest and inside it were scores of walking sticks with gold and silver handles. "Why do these people have such one-track minds?" he sighed. While we were engaged in conversation, the bell rang and an orderly came into the room with another vase, to be presented "with thanks" from Colonel X and his family for a successful treatment. After the orderly left, Tschudi threw the vase violently to the ground and it broke into a thousand pieces.

LOOKING FOR A JOB

I wanted to marry. How was I to procure an income? I had a good training in all branches of medicine, even in surgery—I saw no reason why I should not become a country physician. I sent many letters with copies of my credentials, but received no offers. Then I made up my mind that I must try the effect of personal interviews. My first effort along this line was in a neat and quaint village in the Alps near Ischl. I was shown around by the mayor. The doctor's office was appalling; it reeked with the odors of medicines and decay. A clammy coldness permeated the stench. The room looked so uncanny that it might have been the workshop of a sorcerer. At night I was invited to the home of the postmaster to play cards. There I learned that the only diversion in this place was gambling. Every evening I was expected for this purpose at the home of a different family. I balked at such a monotonous existence and went home.

I thought that perhaps I would be able to find a better place near Vienna. In a medical journal I found two vacancies where lodging and a yearly salary were offered for the treatment of the poor. At this time I was still officially in military service, and Tschudi gave me a holiday. I arrived at the station early and there I met a second candidate, a good-hearted chap, tall and placid as a giraffe, but otherwise ungifted. As there were two vacancies we decided to leave everything to fate. On leaving the station my colleague noticed a tiny cemetery. "How can a physician make both ends meet

in a puny place like that?" said the rival applicant.
"Look at the cemetery." I was malicious enough to
reply, "Wait until you work here, they'll have to enlarge the cemetery." We both laughed.

A tall man asked if we were the doctors. He was the
mayor. We went through a clean village, well-kept. He
praised the different amenities of the place, and repeated many times, "The physician has a nice bungalow, a clean operating room, and everything according
to his wishes." I asked why the last doctor left. "Did he
die?" The mayor told us the former doctor had a "large
income, paid in wine"; he had a huge cellar filled with
wine—he never received any other fee. (This place was
famous for its vineyards.) He was not only a physician,
but also a wine merchant. In addition, he was a drunkard. (Many country doctors, disappointed in their ambitions and hopes, are in danger of becoming gamblers
and drunkards.)

"Why did he leave the place if he was so successful?"
we inquired. "This is a funny story," the mayor replied.
"One night some young chaps tarred and feathered
him; in the morning he found himself in the ditch near
his house. The same day he left the village."

The story was not very encouraging, but the mayor
kept on praising the place. Then he invited us to visit
his wine cellar, and gave us little samples to taste. What
I did not know at that time was that his intention was
to intoxicate two inexperienced fellows by mixing different drinks. He did it on purpose, a frequent "joke"
of these rustics. I tasted the different wines, praised the
quality, and my colleague did the same; we left the
cellar and went out. Suddenly my colleague collapsed

and fell down as if struck by lightning. I also felt that, for the first time in my life, I was drunk.

A carriage was waiting to convey us to the second vacancy; my colleague was packed into the carriage by four men. I stayed close to him for fear he would fall out. In a half-hour we arrived at our destination, where we found the mayor and prominent members of the community waiting in a big room. I am ashamed to confess that I behaved not as a physician, but as a fool. I boasted of my knowledge and pounding the table with my sword (I was still in uniform), I told them that I had just invented a new method of curing all diseases. "You can prove your method right here," said the mayor. "My wife is ill and no doctor can help her. Will you try your luck?"

I do not know what kind of a disease she had. A pretty young woman entered and recited her complaints. I went through the motions of an examination, inspected various parts of her body, looked into her eyes, percussed, used the stethoscope, the ophthalmoscope, and what not. Finally I wrote a prescription. Then we left the place, driving to the near-by station. In the train we both sobered up; I was shocked at my impossible behavior, and afraid that I had poisoned the woman. The best thing would have been to go back to this place, but I could not do that; I was in military service. Should I write and advise the woman not to take the medicine? Should I return there in a sober condition to show that in reality I was different? I consulted my superior, Tschudi. He smiled, "Some physicians are at their best when they're drunk; let's face the worst. You'll never get the job anyway."

I was very busy at the hospital and could not get a free day. I lived in fear of being entangled in a lawsuit and deprived of my medical license as a consequence of my disgraceful behavior. However, I decided to remain quiet for the time being.

Two weeks later I received a registered letter from the village, sealed by the mayor. At first I dared not open it. Finally, I plucked up courage and read the letter—I was flabbergasted; it read:

"Dear Dr. Stekel:

You made an excellent impression upon us all. In case you are willing to accept the position, we will increase your salary from three hundred *gulden* to five hundred. As for my wife, she is absolutely cured. You performed a really miraculous cure by your new method. I shall remain your ever-grateful servant. . . ."

It was my first cure and my only "miraculous" one. Should I accept this offer? I felt that I needed some more training in various special branches. At first, I continued my work at Krafft-Ebing's clinic, but I decided to establish my practice, and to use my free time for further study. I was especially interested in the work of Winternitz, a famous hydrotherapist, a pupil of the world-famous Priesnitz. (Priesnitz was a peasant, noted for his success with neurotics, though he used nothing else but water.)

OPENING OF PRACTICE AND MARRIAGE

What specialty should I choose for my practice? I jokingly remarked that I would like to have my shingle

read "Specialist in All Branches of Medicine." I was
well trained in the treatment of ear, nose, and throat
diseases, and so I started as a specialist in this branch.
My shingle was up, my treatment room was the bedroom of my future parents-in-law. A screen hid their
beds. I had some of the necessary instruments and I
waited for my first patient. No patient came, however,
and so I used the spare time to study with Winternitz.
He was a wonderful man, independent, a master of a
wide medical range. I studied hydrotherapy and mas-
sage, and soon I was proficient in both. My most ardent
desire was to cure neurotics. At Krafft-Ebing's I had
worked with hypnosis and electricity, and now I hoped
to find in the water therapy the long sought panacea. I
had some success, but it was not fully satisfactory.

I took down my shingle as a specialist and started
working as a general practitioner. In the neighborhood
a very well-known practitioner died. I had often noticed that a long wire was drawn from his window to
the street with an inscription behind the handle on the
wall: "Doctor's Bell." In these quarters I could perhaps
get my first patients. Malvina's parents rented this much
larger flat with two separate rooms for the young
couple. They also provided the bedroom furniture.
Malvina and I made our final preparations for our
wedding.

Opposite our building there was a synagogue; it
would have been so simple to cross the street and be
married. However, Malvina's father, poor though he
was, chose a remote synagogue because then we could
drive to the wedding in carriages. How this old man
obtained the means for this extravagance, only the Lord

knows. We and our entourage rode to the distant synagogue; there was a choir and all the pageantry of a
solemn ceremony. I felt sorry for the expense; in vain
I had tried to persuade the old folks to save the money
and to let us be married in a modest manner at some
quaint and simple place. The vanity of these plain
people overcame my resistance.

We spent the two-day honeymoon in a hotel in
Vienna. We visited theatres and museums and on the
third day we came back to begin our new life.

Soon the "Doctor's Bell" rang. A patient had arrived!
He was a shabby old man. He waited fifteen minutes
while I noisily shifted books and opened and shut desk
drawers in the office. He, at least, would be sure that I
was busy. Alas! He was not a patient. He was an erst-
while country doctor who now sought charity. The second "patient" was the "widow of a physician," and the
third "patient" was another "former physician." All
three moved me so much that I gave each a *gulden*.

I did not know that there were many fakers who took
advantage of the naïveté of a newly-established physician. I complained about my disappointing visitors to
a colleague who was twenty years my senior and wise
to the problems of office practice. He chortled. "One
of them came to me, too. I asked him to show his
diploma. He had lost it. My second question was:
'Where is the *sella turcica?*'[1] He had not the slightest
idea. 'What! You call yourself a physician,' I shouted,
'and you don't know where this important fossa is? Get
out!' "

---

[1] Part of the base of the skull. A groove which contains the pituitary
gland.—*The Editor.*

The next day I had the opportunity to use this ruse. In my waiting room some member of the family was always playing the part of a patient. An empty waiting-room disappoints the patients. But the trick may backfire. My neighbor, Dr. Q., an oculist, used his old father for this purpose. A patient, who had not visited the office in two years, returned. "You unfortunate man!" he cried. "You are *still* in treatment?"

The older physicians advised me not to wait for patients, but to hurry along the street with my satchel as though I were answering an urgent call. While I thought this a good suggestion, I preferred to devote my many free hours to Winternitz's lectures. Once, about two years later when I was summoned to an urgent case, I hurried down the street and met the colleague who had given me the advice on "advertising." He wanted to chat. "No time," I answered. "I must rush."

"Incredible," he rebuked me as I hastened past him. "It was I who taught you how to play the role of a busy doctor and now you want to work this trick on me."

My first real patient proved to me that the best clinical training is not always an adequate preparation for practice. I had seen many interesting and complicated cases, but I had not learned enough about everyday diseases such as an upset stomach. My patient, a young servant, was brought by her mistress for treatment of a facial rash. I was taken aback; I examined her for more than half-an-hour. I even entertained a suspicion of venereal disease. Eventually, I concluded it was an irritation from some external source, perhaps from the fire while the girl cooked. I prescribed an ointment, and

I ordered her to return to my office in two days. She did not show up. Three weeks later she met me in the street and laughed at me. "You had better ask for a refund of the money you spent on your education. My rash was the beginning of measles."

I was ashamed. Six years of study and I had not recognized a case of measles! Because of the peculiarity of my curriculum, I had been under no obligation at that time to study pediatrics or dermatology. I had worked for a few months in the children's clinic of the famous pediatrician, Kassowitz, but—by a rare coincidence—had not seen a single case of measles.

Soon, I cursed the bell I had taken over from the deceased doctor. It gave me my first night patients, but also a great deal of annoyances. Many times I was torn from the arms of my wife. One night I was called to a man who had tried to kill himself by drinking lysol. I washed out his stomach and he recovered. On every anniversary of that day he came with his children and brought us flowers. He believed that that night had been the turning point in his life for, after previously having experienced many failures, he later became successful and happy to be alive. "Children," he would say, "look at this doctor very carefully; he saved my life, and you must be grateful to him." At the time he could not pay me, but he gave me his only treasure, an intriguing bust carved by his brother, a promising sculptor, who had died prematurely.

I treated poor patients without a fee. At that time I was ashamed to accept money or to send a bill. I felt it did not correspond with the ideal vocation of a physician. Once a very wealthy man did not pay me although

I had sent him a bill. I once saw him on the street and thinking he might feel ashamed, I crossed to the other side to avoid meeting him.

I never had a fancy to become rich. Therefore, advantage was taken of me by many people, even by some of my publishers; people often believed that I received a large income from my books which are read the world over. Such is not the case. I mentioned that in money matters I was not unlike my father. I never counted my daily receipts and never kept an account of my expenses; but somehow I instinctively arranged my expenses according to my means, and thus never suffered from lack of funds.

At the beginning of my marriage, my wife told me reproachfully that one of my colleagues had a yearly income of twenty thousand *gulden*. At this time I was earning enough for our modest expenses. I looked at her in astonishment. "Is there anything you need?" I asked. "I don't envy that man, I envy no one." It was some months later when she asked me for something that was above my means. "Wait," I told her, "until I earn a little more money. You see things are getting better and better." She lost her self-control and called me a miser. I was horrified. No one has ever accused me of being penurious. When I married her I had to renounce many promising pursuits. I deemed it the greatest sacrifice that I had given up my career with Krafft-Ebing which would have meant, apart from its social advantages, financial security. My wife's reproach, therefore, hurt me deeply. As time went on, it appeared as though I had forgotten her incisive words. Yet they had penetrated and become fixed in my "id." Many things that happened later may have been due to a desire to avenge this unwarranted insult. I wanted to forget it, but the id drove me to decisions I usually would not have made.

JOYS AND WOES OF GENERAL PRACTICE

The welcome ringing of my night bell assured me of enough earnings for necessary expenses and we saved some money toward a home of our own. A friend of my brother loaned us the money to buy furniture, linen, and a piano. In a short time, I repaid him and also met the installments on my military scholarship. It was not difficult to meet my financial obligations as I was getting a reputation and acquiring more and more patients. I published my first medical paper, *Coitus in Children.* This paper was written independently of Freud. In it, I made use of my experiences and, to some extent, the experiences of my friends. Later, I pioneered the discovery that a definite connection existed between acute sore throat and rheumatism. I also published various papers on migraine, influenza, and other current medical problems.

My success in general practice soon made me popular. I even treated effectively some cases of complicated consumption. My principal concept in treating tuberculars was: "Why send the patient away from his home city? He will have to work in Vienna. Therefore he must be cured in Vienna." I gave him a separate room, ordered that the windows be kept open, and employed compresses and various hydrotherapeutic measures. I also obtained notable results with powerful drugs. Perhaps the fact that I devoted much time to these people, that I asked each patient about his life and his conflicts, that I gave him new hope, and tried to allay the worries about his family, contributed to this success. Later, I learned that the psychic component plays a formidable part in tuberculosis. Many people become ill because they are tired of life and have a wish to die. Many years later in Davos, Switzerland, a famous lung specialist said to me, "I think you should treat all my patients."

The practitioner often has to fight the stupidity and the stubbornness of the patient's family as well as the disease. I had a colleague who, as a medical student, had to take every examination several times; he had not the slightest idea of medicine. Later we were all astonished to see that this man became a prominent success as a practitioner. How did he become popular? He came to a patient and after five minutes he announced that he knew the name of the disease. When the diagnosis was wrong, he said that the real disease was a complication of the one he had detected.

At the start of my medical career I imagined that poor people who are treated free of charge are quite grateful. Soon I discovered that these patients are all dominated by the idea that they would be treated in a better manner if they could pay. Later, in my own clinic, even poor patients had to pay according to their means, sometimes as little as twenty *groschen,* for then the treatment was more successful.

On the ingratitude of patients I could fill large volumes. Studying this question, I came to the conclusion that ingratitude is a human quality. There is nothing more difficult to bear than obligation towards another human being. "Ingratitude is the independence of the soul" is a French proverb. It is correct. Grateful patients are a moving exception.

I could tell of many cases, but I will mention only one. I had been called to the feverish child of a poor porter, and after a thorough examination I wrote out a prescription. The woman asked me what the disease was. "I cannot say," I answered, "we shall see tomorrow. Give him a spoonful of the medicine every hour."

"But I have no money to buy the medicine," she complained. I gave her a *gulden*. This was in the morning. That evening I said to myself, if you don't make a second visit, the woman will think it is because she is not able to pay. So I returned, climbed four stories, and went into the room; but before examining the child I noticed a prescription written by the ignorant colleague I have already mentioned. This woman had used my money to call in a "better" physician.

MARITAL CLOUDS

Before long I had to hire a dogcart, for sometimes I had twenty or more calls a day. We moved from the slums, from the old and dilapidated building, into a modern corner house. I was now an established and esteemed physician.

Every practitioner has days in which he has much spare time. I used this free time to visit museums. I did more; I spent a whole holiday in Vienna as though I were an outsider; and I used a guide book which di-

rected me to the curiosities. In the town where one
works, one seems unable to find the time necessary to
view the many points of interest. One delays the visit,
and permits fantasies and irrelevant matters to occupy
the free hours. Fantasies destroy reality. I went into all
the little galleries and in one I was asked to write my
name in the visitor's book. The official looked at the
entry, saw that I was from Vienna, and laughed. "I
haven't seen a visitor from Vienna in my gallery for
two years."

My knowledge of architecture was slight, but with
my guide book I studied the structural details of palaces.
I could go to remote corners of the city and come upon
wondrous, old Viennese courts, whose existence was
unknown to most of the city's residents.

My family life was peaceful; I regretted only that my
wife stopped playing duets, and that she preferred the
society of garrulous, illiterate women, and that I was
forced to accompany her to coffee-houses where I
played cards in order to avoid the boring gossip of these
people. But I must confess that playing cards served as
a mental narcotic; it afforded escape from the gradually
emerging dissonance of our marriage.

The critical time of every marriage is the period when
the couple begins to weary of each other, when they do
not suffice each other and have a craving for other com-
pany. It is then that we witness a phenomenon which is
so characteristic of our time: the flight from the home.
I feel that many modern people have lost something
precious and irreplaceable, the feeling for home. Our
city homes are not built individually. One does not feel

comfortable at home. Immense coffee-houses, noisy
bars, elegant restaurants, and aristocratic clubs lure
people away from home life and into other groups.

To travel had always been my innermost drive. I
wanted to wander, to climb mountains, to see new landscapes. The first holiday with my wife was like an en-
chanting dream. We walked all day and I was never so
much in love with her as after a tiring hike on a mountain. It is not true that fatigue interferes with sexual
passion, although many people pretend fatigue in order
to avoid embraces.

The second holiday in the Dolomites brought me a
bitter disappointment. My wife preferred to see nature
from a comfortable car, while I wanted to tire myself
out, to wander with a heavy knapsack on my shoulders.
In the midst of the holiday, in which I did my mountain climbing alone, she told me, "I feel sick" and I had
to nurse her for a week in one of the most beautiful
parts of Italy.

This flight into illness was repeated on the next two
holidays; but I was still a model husband, avoiding
every quarrel. I always gave in to the small demands of
the day, so that our acquaintances often made fun of
me and called me "As you like, my child."

One summer we rented a bungalow in a holiday resort near Vienna, and I used to ride on my bicycle to
and from the city every day. I was an ardent cyclist,
and never became tired. My first pamphlet was called
Health and the Bicycle; it comprised a collection of
items I had published every week in a Sunday paper.
One evening I found three gentlemen who shared the
same bungalow with us, waiting for me at the gate. They

As a Young Physician

complained that their hitherto peaceful marriages had grown unhappy, and that I was responsible. "You are too submissive," they said. "Our wives are beginning to rebel and constantly hint at your example as a model husband. You will have to act more like a man."

FLIGHT TO THE MOUNTAINS

Behind my slavish obedience to my wife's wishes must have been hidden a strong internal defiance. For one day I went to her and stated very firmly and without any introduction, "Tomorrow I am going on a trip, and you will not see me for three weeks." At first she could not find words. My pronouncement took her completely by surprise. Finally she tried reproaches and tears, but they did not move me. I packed my knapsack and left that same night on a sleeping car to a lake in Carinthia. The morning I arrived I developed severe pains in my legs and could barely move them. I went to the lake with the thought that perhaps sunshine and swimming would relieve me; but the pains persisted. I limped slowly to the druggist, but it was then the noon hour and the shop would be closed until two o'clock. For nearly two hours I waited on a bench, writhing in pain. I understand now that these pains actually represented internal reproaches and self-punishment because I had left my wife against her will.

Finally, at two o'clock, the druggist opened his shop. I bought aspirins and took two tablets, a whole gram. At four o'clock I took the train to a place in Tyrol; at the beginning of the journey I still felt pain, but it

became less and less as I traveled, and it was completely
absent when I left the train. I walked until nightfall
when I came to a hostel where I spent the night. The
next day I started to climb the Grossglockner. By
evening I reached a hut near the glacier. Darkness had
fallen. The general room was crowded with about
thirty tourists, most of whom were former students.
Soon we were all drinking, and then I led the singing.
Our gleeful voices enlivened the hut and the white soli-
tude beyond. I was always able to entertain a crowd,
and so it was late when we went to bed.

I went to Switzerland and to Italy. Every moment of
my trip was enjoyed to the full. I was now sunburned
and strong, and with my wild beard and big alpine cane
I looked like a brigand. I arrived at Maloja, a place
which brought many recollections of the philosopher
Nietzsche and the painter Segantini. There were three
waitresses at the hotel, each more beautiful than the
other. In my mind I called this place the "Hotel of the
Pretty Girls." Next day I set out on the long route to
Italy. No one asked for a passport at the border. How
different from the present universal suspicion and sur-
veillance.

During the whole trip I wrote only two short post-
cards home. I have described in my books the phenomenon that I call "annulment." It is not the same as
repression. Freud's "Little Hans" had repressed all his
recollections of the time he went to Freud, but there
must have remained traces in his mind. In annulment
there is a conscious blindness. During the trip I went
through an annulment in regard to my marriage. I felt

as though I were a bachelor. I acted accordingly, but if someone had asked me, "Are you married?" I would have answered, "Of course I am."

HOME AGAIN—CHILDREN'S SONGS

When I came home, my wife was easily appeased. I continued my work and spent much time with my children. I had never liked the cruel fairy tales of Grimm, so I invented fairy tales for my children, and they preferred mine to some I read from a book. I started to train their musical ears very early. I purchased some volumes of children's songs, but the children did not like them very much, so I composed my own songs, both the music and simple words. The little children were enraptured. The children of the neighbors came in to join us, and in a short time we had a chorus. All of the songs were improvised. When I came home the children would climb over me and say, "Daddy, please make a new song."

I mentioned before that I did not strive for success and publicity. Everything came my way. One day a famous singer came, a lady who had heard of my children's songs and said she would like to use them in a recital for children. I copied the best ones for her and later heard her sing them at a concert—a new experience for me. I was pleased also when the audience enjoyed my songs. Some months later, there was a children's day in Vienna. Great preparations were made, and among them was a recital in the largest concert hall. Frau

Hilgermann, of the Vienna Opera had been invited to sing. She came to see me and chose several of my songs to sing on this occasion, and we rehearsed them together. I accompanied her on the piano at the concert. One of the songs had to be repeated three times. Thus the songs went from hand to hand, were used in recitals and children's choirs, and it happened that the English publisher, Bosworth, who was the manager of the Vienna branch of his firm, heard these songs and had them published in three volumes. They became very popular. Imagine my impressions when sometimes, passing by an open window, I could hear a child singing one of my songs. One of them became the favorite of a charming Viennese singer who often sang it at recitals for grownups. Later, a recording was made of this song. Many parents still use my songs for their children without knowing that the words and music are by Stekel, the psychoanalyst. I am sorry they are not translated into English. One patient of mine translated some of them but I did not urge him to finish the job, and did not look for a publisher, and so nothing materialized.

At this time I published a poem, "Resignation," in which I accepted the fate of an average man. I maintained a large practice, published some medical papers, played the piano, enjoyed my string quartet, read some good books and put on weight. I became rather potbellied. In the afternoon I played cards—in short, I was well on the way to becoming a Philistine.

My plan for writing the novel *Fettered Titans* was given up. I became disappointed with my work as a physician; I felt that it is Nature that heals or kills, that medical practice in itself is monotonous—that the same diseases recur over and over. Even the patients are sometimes untrustworthy, and when they are benefited by the doctor, they are often ungrateful. So I reduced my life to the natural needs, and lost some of my former idealism.

Chapter Four

INTRODUCTION TO FREUD
AND PSYCHOANALYSIS

★

THROUGH MY PUBLICATIONS I met many interesting people. One day a journalist who was on the staff of a
leading daily came into my office. In the course of our
conversation he told me that his newspaper was looking
for a medical man who could write popular items. The
physician who had performed the assignment had died,
and the readers desired that the column be continued.
I remembered that I had once written an article, *Between Disease and Health,* which had lain in a drawer
for two years. I gave him the manuscript and after three
days I saw myself in print on the first page of the newspaper. It was the custom in Austria to divide the first
page into two parts, the upper part mostly for politics,
the under part for science and art. This lower part was
called the feuilleton. A clever man once made an aphorism: "The feuilleton is the contemporary variant of
the ancient 'writer's' itch." (I once had to look through
the galleyproof of a work written by Krafft-Ebing, and

he said to me, "Should you ever become infected with the printer's ink, you will never recover!")

I wrote for this paper every week, then for others, received good fees, and became popular. I had many admirers who wrote to the papers if my material failed to appear in even one issue. Some of the articles were published in my books. I received letters from all parts of Austria, some very amusing. Thus, I also came into contact with many prominent literary men.

Among them was a high-spirited physician, Kahane. He had the same fate as myself: he was extremely gifted, and renounced—I don't know why—the academic career; he worked in an institution where he treated neurotic patients with electricity. He mentioned a name new to me—that of Sigmund Freud, then "Docent" or assistant professor, lecturing once a week at the university. These lectures, Kahane told me, were original, packed with new ideas. He informed me that Freud had quoted my paper on *Coitus in Children*, and had mentioned that he would like to get in touch with me. I shouldn't miss the opportunity.

I have previously referred to my interest in "neuroses," as they were then called. I was very disappointed to find that some cases proved incurable, for neither electricity nor hydrotherapy seemed to be effective. Sometimes, while still unaware of Freud's research and methods, I had asked such persons about frustrated ambitions, and about their sex life. It never entered my head that the "nervous" man does not know where the shoe pinches. I did not know about the unconscious, I did not know that the most important facts buried in the unconscious are revealed by dreams.

I was not interested in dreams. Twice I had incestuous dreams about my mother, and consoled myself with the reflection that Caesar and Alexander the Great had similar dreams. The interpreter explained to Alexander that the mother was a symbol of the earth and that to "sleep with the mother" meant to conquer the earth. I also had homosexual dreams, but at that time I had not even an inkling of sexology and did not know that all human beings are bisexual. In a weekly paper I read a long and witty review of Freud's then newly published work, *The Interpretation of Dreams.* The reviewer found the book abstruse and unscientific. I have already mentioned my skepticism about reviews. I decided to call on Freud. He lent me his new book. I was enraptured. I wrote a long paper in two parts in the "Neues Wiener Tagblatt" and emphasized the importance of this book which was inaugurating a new science of dream interpretation. It was the first favorable appreciation of this outstanding work which started a new era in psychology and mental healing. Freud was much pleased and dedicated a volume to me, with the words, "With best thanks to my colleague Stekel for his appreciation." The books and my talks with Freud were like sunshine after rain. At last I had learned the right method of curing neurotics. Many obscure cases in my practice ceased to be enigmas. I had a large and ever-replenished reservoir of material, and it was a pleasure to find the correctness of Freud's observations confirmed by many cases that hitherto I had not been able to understand. The fact that I was a practitioner was an advantage in that it enabled me to study a vast quantity of patients who had the most diverse disorders. I wrote numerous articles about Freud and was one of the first to recognize the greatness of this genius. Wittels writes in his book on Freud:[1] "The printing machines of Europe sighed under the burden of the papers Stekel wrote on Freud." I was the apostle of Freud who was my Christ!

The editors of "Tagblatt," the newspaper in which I published my "feuilletons," once requested that I write at least one article without mentioning Freud.

The publisher Knepler proposed that I prepare a booklet on appendicitis. At that time there was an excessive fear of this disease. Even normal people had preventive appendectomies. I have always believed that there is no superfluous organ in the human body, but that we do not understand the purpose of some organs. I wrote my pamphlet, *Appendicitis Without End.* It was a best-seller.

I was now becoming a prolific writer. My next pamphlet was *The Causes of Nervousness* followed by a series of pamphlets. They were translated into several languages. In *Abstinence and Health,* the exaggerated fear regarding the consequences of masturbation was submitted to a careful scrutiny for the first time. The leading idea of the study was that what had hitherto erroneously been considered a detrimental effect of masturbation was actually the result of a mental conflict created by the much-maligned sexual activity. The popular brochure later became the starting point of a larger book, *Onanie und Homosexualität* (Masturba-

---

[1] *Sigmund Freud: His Personality, His Teachings, and His School.* Translated by Eden and Cedar Paul, London, Allen and Unwin, Ltd., 1924.

tion and Homosexuality) which was published by Urban and Schwarzenberg in Vienna. Its third edition appeared in 1923.[2] *Masturbation and Homosexuality* had the mission of doing away with two dangerous psychiatric superstitions; namely, that masturbation is harmful and that homosexuality is incurable.

ANALYSIS WITH FREUD

When I first visited Freud, I had some sexual problems and wanted to consult him as an authority on sex. I have already mentioned that Freud knew my study on *Coitus in Children*. He wrote in his article on *Etiology of Hysteria* (Wiener Klin. Rundschau, 1896) as follows: "It appears certain that our children are exposed to sexual aggressions much more frequently than one would expect in view of the lack of attention to this problem shown by parents in general. In my attempt to ascertain what, if anything, is known on this subject, I learned from colleagues that a number of publications by pediatricians have appeared, in which nurses and nurse-maids were accused of various sexual transgressions toward children and even infants. In the last few weeks I came across a study written by Dr. Stekel in Vienna, which deals with the 'Coitus in Children.' "

I felt I could approach Freud with confidence. He suggested psychoanalysis.

My treatment lasted not more than eight sessions. I

2 The first part of this work, *Auto-Erotism,* was published in the English language by the Liveright Publishing Corporation, New York, 1950. The second part divided into two volumes, *Bisexual Love* and *The Homosexual Neurosis,* appeared in 1929 published by Emerson Books, Inc., New York.—*The Editor.*

told Freud my life history and he expressed his surprise about the fact that I had so few repressions. In one of my dreams he found what he termed a mother fixation. I could not believe it. The few incestuous dreams I had had before appeared to me as normal human manifestations.

Freud also mentioned on one occasion that since I had so few repressions regarding my own early sex life, I was an invaluable witness for his theory of infantile sex.

ABBAZIA

At that time, in my general practice, I still had many night calls and often had to brave wind and storm. Once I was caught in a chilly rain without the proper clothing for such weather. The result was an attack of pleurisy. For the first time since my typhoid I was confined to my bed. I had excruciating pains. My friend and teacher, Professor Nothnagel, used an old method; he applied some leeches—and the pain vanished as if by magic. Nevertheless, I had a pleural effusion and high temperature, and my family physician told me this pleurisy would last for weeks. I had to stay in bed for more than three weeks. The time seemed endless. I dictated numerous articles to my wife. All were published. I tried to read and to think, but for one of my active temperament the enforced idleness was like a prison. Suddenly a vision of the ocean, of sunshine, flashed before me. I said to myself, "You will overcome this disease by getting out in the sun." I wanted to travel to Abbazia, at that time an Austrian seashore resort, but now in Italy.[3]

---

3 Today Abbazia belongs to Yugoslavia.—*The Editor.*

My physician warned me against this trip, but Nothnagel was in favor of it. He thought that the change of air, the sunshine, and the new impressions might effect a cure. I took Nothnagel's advice. My wife wanted to accompany me, but this was beyond my modest means. On the night before leaving I had a dream.

I heard a voice warning me: "You will live only a fortnight. Use your time!"

Despite this strange dream I stuck to my plan. After a comfortable night in the sleeping compartment, I arrived, early in the morning, in Abbazia. It was a beautiful day, with a clear sky and bright sunshine, but I had such a shivering spell that I had to go to bed. There I lay for an hour in a desperate frame of mind. I longed to see the ocean and to enjoy the sunshine. Again I heard an inner call in the form of a dream.

Someone said: "Only the sun will cure you."

I dressed and went out, slowly, haltingly, from the boarding house to the beach. At last I was by the sea, on a sunny bench; the impression was not overly-inspiring because in front of Abbazia lies an island. I was in a bay and it was impossible to see the expanse of the ocean. But for me it was a thrilling event. For a whole hour I was lost in dreamy observation. Then I walked very cautiously along the winding boardwalk. I soon came to a house where I saw the shingle of a doctor who had been recommended to me as the best of the local physicians. He was at home. He made a thorough examination and was horrified. "You are careless and foolhardy to walk about with a high temperature and a big effusion in the left pleura. Go back to bed. Apply cold compresses. Change them every hour. I'll send you a man who will wash you every morning. Keep on the diet I will prescribe. I will visit you."

His injunctions were hard to accept. Had I come to Abbazia to lie in bed? In the afternoon I sat for some hours in the sunshine, and that night I went to bed early. Next morning the man came to wash me and to rub my body, and he repeated the doctor's warning that I must stay in bed. It was a splendid day. I followed my instinct and went to my beloved bench. I took short walks and felt much better as I went from one bench to another. I was in the open all day. The next morning I paid the man who washed me and stopped further treatment. I improved every day, and in a short time I was able to walk for two or three hours without any pain, and without fatigue. After a week I went back to my colleague; he examined me and then exclaimed: "What! No temperature? And the effusion has been absorbed. What did you do to produce this miracle?"

I confessed that I had not followed his instructions, that I had taken long walks. He repeated his warning, but I knew that my treatment was concluded.

Every afternoon little steamers went out on excursions to nearby islands. I made use of this opportunity—stretched out in a comfortable deck-chair, in wind and sunshine. I indulged in daydreams, and it was then that I began to understand the reasons for my illness and to admit that diseases sometimes serve an unconscious purpose. Thanks to my illness I had gone on a delightful holiday, and acquired a new passion, the sea. This passion became so strong that I toyed with the idea of spending the largest part of each year on a yacht as soon as I became wealthy. In later years I made several voyages. I was never seasick, and I sometimes envied the ship's doctors for being able to practice at sea. May I confess the only recurring wish fantasy of mine? I believed that a rich American would come to me one day and say: "Dr. Stekel, you have worked enough. May I propose a year on my yacht as a vacation for you?" I am sorry to say, he never came, this kindly American!

According to the portentous dream I had just before leaving Vienna, my death was at hand. Here on Abbazia the fourteenth day was arriving. I had become acquainted with an intelligent young baron who was staying at our boarding house, and I asked him to write to Freud about my dream if I should die. Freud did not believe in telepathic and prophetic dreams. The baron was superstitious. At my words he made the sign of the cross several times and begged me to remain indoors.

I defied fate and went to a town opposite Fiume by boat to visit an old castle. A storm broke. Black clouds rushed across the sky. The *bora,* an awesome thunder storm from the north, struck. The boat was thrown from side to side as though it were a nutshell. The craft was in imminent danger of capsizing. None of us expected to reach the protective harbor. The captain's face betrayed his anxiety, and the passengers flopped and floundered in their seasickness. I climbed the rigging of the foremast and contemplated the spectacle with detached curiosity. Had the dream of doom been right? A wave reared high above the vessel, smashed over the bow, and drenched me with stinging, salty spray. How gently it washed the deck as it receded, and the staggering and quivering boat steadied itself! No more such waves attacked us. The trip which normally took three-quarters of an hour, lasted two hours. We finally reached the harbor where a red balloon gave warning that boat trips were forbidden. The *bora* increased its ferocity. A wave hurled itself over the promenade. I hurried to my quarters and changed into dry clothes.

A week later I went home. I was better. But after a few weeks I had to go back to Abbazia to resume convalescence; and I stayed there for two months. When I again returned to Vienna I was a healthy man.

OH, THESE DOCTORS!

I was agreeably surprised to learn that, although my absence had been long, I had lost none of my patients. Their loyalty moved me, and later became a source of embarrassment when I was about to give up general practice. I had arranged for a reputable and talented doctor to take over my practice during my leave. But what happened? The doctor who minded my patients removed their tonsils or operated on them for appendicitis. He sent others to the rhinologist. During my entire practice I had not seen such a high proportion of operations among the patients of a general practitioner. Later I discovered the solution to the riddle. My substitute was an adherent of dichotomy. The French author, Gyp, has described this practice in her book, *Oh,— ces bons Docteurs!* It would seem that prolific and even indiscriminate scalpel wielding was by no means confined to my own environment. I need not emphasize

DR. SIGMUND FREUD

that I never abused the confidence of my patients in such an unworthy manner. As in any profession, among doctors there are some who are greedy for money, some who are merchants rather than healers, thinking more of their profits than of the well-being of their patients. Even some well-known professors were more interested in financial gain than in their cases. One professor whom I had called in for consultation tried to give me some money. Some doctors used to get fees as "assistants" at operations, though they never assisted.

Later it occasionally happened that a physician would bring me a patient and would ask for a share of the fee. I always refused such demands, and in this way lost a few wealthy patients. In Vienna there were professional touts who waited at the stations and picked out likely-looking people; they introduced themselves as "guides" and brought these persons to physicians from whom they received a commission. I must state here that a big majority of physicians are truly idealistic persons. But where there is light there is shadow.

WORKING WITH FREUD

I do not know exactly when I began to analyze. It might have been in 1903. I knew that a certain Dr. Rudolf Reitler had tried this method at that time. I think he was the first to apply Freud's theories in practice. A staunch supporter of Freud, he remained faithful to him until his death.

Though in my private practice I had conducted a

number of minor analyses, my first more important case was referred to me by Freud. It was the case of the rabbi published in my book on *Anxiety States.*

The case of the rabbi was very interesting: The forty-two-year-old patient had been suffering for the last six years from the fear of losing the trend of his thoughts and "getting stuck" while delivering his sabbath sermon. He also displayed other symptoms, such as stuttering and feeling of heat in arms and legs (paresthesias) when he had to give counsel in religious matters, activities in which he excelled.

Analysis revealed a sibling rivalry toward his brother. After their father's death the patient's brother received a large sum of money, while the patient inherited a valuable collection of rabbinical books. After his brother squandered his money he laid claim to some of the patient's books. Standing in front of his bookshelves the patient exclaimed: "I shall not let a single book *out of my hands!* You will have to take me from my books by force!" This declaration later evoked a strong feeling of guilt.

During analysis the patient maintained for a long time that he did not know anything about sex until his wedding night when his mother enlightened both bride and groom about marital relations. However, dreams led me to the discovery of important details of the patient's sexual life. The sexton in his father's house induced the patient to all sorts of sexual games, including fellatio, which he performed on the patient while the latter was holding the man's penis in his hand. The patient also masturbated a great deal, alone and with his brother.

The patient was unquestionably faithful to his wife but he was exposed to many sexual wish fantasies. On one occasion he committed a transgression of his strict religious code by shaking hands with an attractive woman. He felt as if a hot current were flowing through his arm. A temporary loss of feeling resulted. He was afraid of God's punishment for his sinful thoughts.

The analysis revealed that the patient's arm paresthesias were determined: (1) by his masturbation, (2) by his homosexual experiences (holding the sexton's penis), and (3) by the vow about the books. His stuttering during his official functions occurred whenever sexual thoughts obtruded into his conscious mind and thus disturbed his solemnly devout mood. He confessed that the letters of the Hebrew word "Adonai" (Our Lord) frequently associated themselves in his mind with a vision of intercourse and that his attempt to suppress this sexual fantasy invariably led to a confusion of his thoughts.

After overcoming various resistances, the analysis made good progress and ended with a clear success. I began to feel more confident in the field of psychotherapy—a new world was opened to me.

I visited Freud frequently, reported on my observations, and received innumerable stimulations from him. He also began to supply me with patients.

I, in turn, used my newspaper contacts as outlets for the new science, and fought for Freud's theories in every possible way.

Gradually I became known as a collaborator of Freud. I gave him the suggestion of founding a little discussion group; he accepted the idea, and every Wednesday evening after supper we met in Freud's home. I am the only surviving original member of the circle. In addition to Freud and myself, there were the physicians Max Kahane, Rudolf Reitler, and Alfred Adler. (Adler later denied that he was a pupil of Freud and showed a postcard as proof. The card was the one which invited him to our group's first meeting. But is it not significant that he kept this post-card so many years?)

These first evenings were inspiring. We found some random themes to talk about, and everybody participated in a real discussion. On the first night we spoke about the psychological implications of smoking. There was complete harmony among the five, no dissonances; we were like pioneers in a newly discovered land, and Freud was the leader. A spark seemed to jump from one mind to the other, and every evening was like a revelation. We were so enthralled by these meetings that we decided new members could be added to our circle only by unanimous consent. The new ones came: Paul Federn and Edward Hitschmann, later Isidor Sadger who introduced Fritz Wittels.

It was then that fate again intervened and another opportunity presented itself. In a Berlin paper, I had published an article on anxiety states. Shortly thereafter I received a letter from the editor of a Berlin medical journal asking me if I would write an article for physicians. I consented. I wrote the article, and a week later I received a letter from a book publisher asking me if I would write a book on anxiety states. I had gathered so much material in my practice that I immediately accepted the offer and began the book.

My work as a psychotherapist became a tremendous

joy to me. I had the conviction that at last I had discovered my true vocation. Often I encountered an
enigma and took recourse to my intuitive faculty in
order to solve an otherwise insoluble problem. In many
cases I was able to guide the patient toward a new life.
Yet my vocation had its seamy side. I could treat only
patients who awakened my interest, and with whom I
felt sympathetic. (Paracelsus was right in saying, "The
only thing we doctors can give our patients is our love.")
I soon dismissed patients who did not appeal to me, or
turned them over to my pupils. When the patient bored
me it was a torment, and I often had to fight against a
strong desire to fall asleep. During the World War,
when all of us were undernourished, I was treating the
daughter of a wealthy banker. I found her such an in-
fernal bore that, although I was in strained circumstances (like all the others, except the war-profiteers),
I simply could not continue the analysis. Session after
session I found myself looking at the clock to see if the
allotted time was nearly over.

Once I had undertaken the treatment of an elderly
lady whose son I had cured. She, naturally, had confidence in me. Her flow of speech was like a waterfall.
One hot summer afternoon sleep overcame me in the
midst of the session. When I awoke, the lady had vanished—and, of course, I never saw her again. After this
incident I grew more cautious and invariably insisted
upon a trial week before agreeing to undertake a complete analysis. One of my reasons was to find out if
success was probable; but I also wanted to know whether
my interest in the case and my sympathetic feeling
toward the patient would suffice to carry me through.

NERVOUS ANXIETY STATES

I began to work on my first scientific book. As a general practitioner I had occasion to see a much more variegated material than the average clinician. I made a plan for the development of my book. I decided to divide the volume into three parts. The first part would be concerned with all the manifestations of anxiety through organic diseases. I called this part "The Organ-Language of the Mind." The second part was to describe phobias, and the third part was to present my general views on morbid fear.

I spoke about this plan to Freud, and he promised to write a preface. He imposed one condition. We should go through the whole book together, lest I should write something that was not in accordance with his theory. So I came to his house every Sunday, and we went through the book, chapter by chapter; he clarified some parts and added others. He gave many suggestions. I did not dare to oppose him.

I could not write the introduction to the chapter on "Anxiety Hysteria." Freud himself wrote the first two-and-a-half pages of the second part of my book as an introduction.

After the second part was finished, I received a severe shock from Freud. He advised me to publish only the first part and to withhold the second. "Why?" I asked.

"It will arouse too much opposition, and the effect of the excellent first part will be spoiled," he replied.

I now took recourse to a diplomatic trick. I asked my publisher to state in a letter to me that he could not renounce the publication of the second part. Freud was forced to give in; but he warned me, "It's your book. You will have to bear the consequences. There will be a storm of opposition against you, and it will damage rather than help your work."

Finally the book was finished. I only awaited the preface. When at last I received it from Freud, it was so noncommittal and indifferent, that I had to give it back to him. He gave me a second version, which I likewise had to return. I was determined to publish my book without the preface. However, the third attempt was a little warmer.[1] It ran as follows:

"Investigations on the etiology and the psychic mechanism of neurotic disorders which I have conducted since 1893 and which at first aroused but little interest by our profession, found, at last, recognition by a number of medical scientists. They have drawn attention to the psychoanalytic method of research and therapy on which my conclusions were based. Dr. Wilhelm Stekel, one of the first colleagues whom I was able to introduce to psychoanalysis, and who, because of many years of practical experience, has become familiar with its technique, has undertaken to elaborate a chapter from the clinic of these neuroses on the basis of my views. He will attempt to present to the medical readers his experiences obtained through the application of the psychoanalytical method. While readily accepting the responsibility for his work in the above sense, it appears fair to state expressly that my direct influence upon the book on the nervous anxiety states has been very small. The observations and all the details of concept and interpretation are his own; only the name "Anxiety Hysteria" refers to my own suggestion.

---

[1] Freud, Ges. Schr., Int. Psa. Verlag, Vol. XI, page 239.

I may say that Dr. Stekel's work is based on a rich experience and that it is designated toward stimulating other physicians to verify by their own effort our views on the etiology of these conditions. The book offers in many places unexpected insight into life's realities which may hide behind neurotic symptoms; it will not fail to convince our colleagues that it is not irrelevant for both their understanding and their therapeutic action what attitude they are inclined to take regarding the hints and explanations contained in this book."

I accepted this and the book was published. It was an immediate success. Even opponents of our theories acknowledged that it was worth reading. The prophecy of Freud that there would be a storm of opposition proved to be wrong.

My book bore the title *Nervous Anxiety States and Their Treatment*.[2]

For the first time there was a full description of the organ-language of the mind; many supposedly organic diseases were explained as psychic disorders. It was a textbook for all psychotherapists. Of all my works, this is perhaps my best book, although it was written before many of my discoveries. My experiences as a practitioner and my first cases as a psychoanalyst were presented there. In a short time, the first edition was sold out and I had to work on an enlarged second edition.

My book brought me many patients. Gradually, it

---

[2] "Nervöse Angstzustände und ihre Behandlung," Urban & Schwarzenberg, Berlin and Vienna, 1912. Its fourth edition appeared in 1924. Now published in English by the Liveright Publishing Corp., New York, 1950.—*The Editor*.

became more and more difficult for me to combine general practice and analysis. I consulted Freud, and he promised to help me if I became a specialist. So I made the most important step in my life: I decided to give up general practice and to specialize.

THE GROWTH OF PSYCHOANALYSIS

Meanwhile our circle attracted many new members. Freud's room proved too small and we had to hire a larger room for our meetings. But I am sorry to say that the old harmonious atmosphere vanished. Quarrels among the pupils, discords, and questions of self-esteem replaced the former spirit of close friendship. Feeling disheartened, Freud once complained to me, "When I look at my pupils, I get the impression that psychoanalysis liberates the worst instincts in human beings."

For a long time adherents came only from Vienna; soon they came from all parts of the world, especially from Germany and Switzerland. In a medical paper, Jung wrote a review in which he referred to Freud as the pioneer of a new psychological approach. Freud was very happy about this statement because Jung was the assistant to Bleuler in Zurich. (Bleuler was the successor of the famous Forel and head of the psychiatric clinic in Zurich.) Freud's hope was that he could win over this center of scientific psychiatry. His hopes were realized, for Bleuler soon became one of his ardent disciples. Zurich was the first official medical school which accepted the new psychology.

We decided to arrange an international meeting in Salzburg. There were, altogether, about forty Freudians at this meeting. Among them were Bleuler, Jung, Ferenczi, Abraham, and the first American Freudian, Brill. Each of these physicians later became the leader of a group of psychoanalysts in his own country. Attending the meeting was also the highly gifted Otto Gross. In his inspiring speech he compared Freud to Nietzsche and hailed him as a destroyer of old prejudices, an enlarger of psychological horizons, and a scientific revolutionary. Freud himself gave a stimulating speech on doubt. He explained doubt as the doubt regarding love, and quoted the words of Hamlet:

> *"Doubt thou the stars are fire;*
> *Doubt that the sun doth move;*
> *Doubt truth to be a liar;*
> *But never doubt, I love."*

DECLINE OF MARRIAGE

I now had to move into the city. First of all, the street where I lived was too noisy; secondly, I wanted to free myself of the patients of my general practice. My wife and I quarrelled over this; she believed that I was taking a dangerous and reckless step, that I would reduce the entire family to penury. Partly because of this attitude and partly for other reasons, the gulf between my wife and myself became wider and wider. She was not interested in psychology and once went so far as to state: "I can't go along with you in this matter, it's like a swindle."

I can trace the beginning of our discord to events

which occurred long before this conflict. I have already mentioned that we no longer played duets. At last, the only spiritual world we had in common was that of books. To read the same books and to discuss them was a source of pleasure and an important bond; but soon even this ceased, and we gradually drifted far apart. I should not like to blame my wife; perhaps I was in the wrong. She was a fine woman, but she had so many virtues that I, a man with many faults, must have felt inferior by comparison. My wife always attempted to henpeck me. Usually I gave in, but internally the will-to-submission must have given place to a defiant will-to-power. Something must have been basically wrong in our marital relationship, for it never offered a sense of complete pleasure. As a psychotherapist I could not fail to be aware of a violent internal protest. One day I was no longer a man. I tried everything to overcome my weakness, but I failed. This period lasted two years.

In my new quarters I started work as a psychoanalyst. At times I had to work from morning to night. In the evenings I was tired, glad to have finished my day's work; but I did not reckon with my wife. She would come with a piece of paper on which were notes of calls from my former patients. Although she knew that I had given up general practice, and although I had told her many times to inform the patients that I was not accepting calls, she continued, nevertheless, to accept them.

"Is this an example of your humanity?" she would cry. "Are you a physician or aren't you? Will you let your patients down?"

"There are many other physicians who will be glad to help them," I answered.

"They want only you," she insisted. "They have confidence in you."

What could I do? After a day's hard work, I had to go on visiting many patients.

The psychology of these patients was very interesting. In former times they resented waiting even as much as half an hour, and now they waited patiently and stubbornly all day to see me. A patient said to me, "I'll wait until midnight, but I want only you." It was hard to get rid of these faithful adherents, and often I had to be adamant and cruel as I fought the dictate of my conscience. Finally, I convinced my patients that it was impossible for me to combine the duties of a family physician and those of a specialist.

My work proceeded. Soon the second edition of my book on *Anxiety States* appeared. Its number of pages was twice that of the first edition.

I used my knowledge of poetry and literature to publish a pamphlet, *Poetry and Neurosis*,[1] in which I analyzed a drama of the Austrian poet, Grillparzer. In this pamphlet I attempted to prove that the work of a poet is like a confession expressing his personal conflicts and experiences. It was the first time psychoanalysis was used for comment on a poetic work. My theory, expressed in *Poetry and Neurosis*, was that all poets are neurotics, and that poetry is an abreaction of neurosis.

At this time I also began my first book on dreams.[2] Chapters of the book were published in a yearly periodi-

---

[1] *Dichtung und Neurose,* published by J. F. Bergmann, Wiesbaden, 1913.

[2] *Die Sprache des Traumes,* published by J. F. Bergmann, Wiesbaden, 1911.

cal, whose editor was Jung. I soon became aware of a growing resistance to the acceptance of my papers. As stated before, the former harmony among the Freudians was gone; there was an heir-pretendency and a secret rivalry amongst the pupils. Adler came as a novice to our circle, and at the beginning was so naïve regarding psychoanalysis that he said to me after a meeting, "I would like to go through this great experience! You find the repressed psychic trauma; then the patient jumps up from the couch. He is a different being, cured." We did not know at that time that analysis is, in the main, a task of re-education, and that the first hypothesis of Freud, "Find the psychic trauma and the patient is cured," has been one of the passing fallacies of the early days of psychoanalysis.

All that time psychoanalysts were springing up like mushrooms. They throve in the dark forests of the human psyche. They were all hunting for the basic "trauma." Freud, himself, published a paper, "The History of an Infantile Neurosis"[3] in which he stated that he had found the trauma after three years of analysis. What was the trauma? A three-year-old boy watched his parents having sexual intercourse.

I should like to add here parenthetically that this patient had to be analyzed again, some time later, by one of Freud's pupils; the patient suffered from paranoia. I was informed about this analysis a few years later through a strange coincidence which I should like to report here.

My love of nature was so strong that at the start of

[3] "Aus der Geschichte einer infantilen Neurose," in "Sammlung kleiner Schriften zur Neurosenlehre," Hugo Heller, Vienna, 1918.

my profession as a psychoanalyst I divided my work into two parts. Seven months of the year I worked in Vienna, and five months in Ischl, the beautiful place where the Emperor had his summer home. I loved Ischl and its quiet, almost deserted walks. Many of my patients were foreigners and they enjoyed this quaint place much more than the hot city of Vienna. At the end of April I went to Ischl, where I took a comfortable bungalow with a pretty garden. I worked in the garden for the most part. It is a prejudice to believe that the patient must always lie on the couch and the analyst sit behind him like a hidden god. I had very good results with patients I treated in the open air.

While sitting in my garden at breakfast, or at work, I frequently noticed a lady on a balcony across the street. Some time later I made her acquaintance.

"My name is Mrs. G.," she said. "I have read some of your books and I have always wondered if you live the way you write. I have been watching you for some time and I decided to have a talk with you. I have heard that you treat your patients only a short time . . . a few months, or a little longer. My son has been in analysis with Freud for three years now and has recently received even two sessions a day . . ."

I explained that methods are different, and that every physician chooses a method that suits his individuality. She then told me the story of her son. She also invited me to come to Russia where she owned a large estate. Later, she translated two of my books into Russian.

Chapter Five

THE BREAK WITH FREUD

★

THE CONGRESS IN WEIMAR

THE NEXT Congress was held in Weimar. It was attended by nearly eighty psychotherapists.

While attending this Congress a deluge of history assailed me. I slept in a room where Napoleon had once stayed for a night. But an even stronger impression was received in the room in which there were the coffins of Goethe and Schiller; many garlands of flowers bore witness to the admiration by the living. I gazed at the two coffins. What is glory? What is adoration by posterity? I felt a peculiar upsurge of lust for life. Only a living person is king of his life! Work and enjoy your life! The words of Horace came to mind, *Carpe Diem!* Then I thought of Schiller's famous line, "What you have refused in a moment, no eternity will bring back to you."

The Congress started. I was surprised when Ferenczi (induced by Freud) proposed that Jung should be elected life-time president of the International Analytical Society. Thus he would have the right (among other things) to examine all papers submitted and to decide which he would publish. No analytical paper would be published without his consent.

I was against this motion. I insisted that our new science would go down if it were not absolutely free. I mentioned how difficult it had been to place our first papers in the medical journals. If a life-time president had to be elected, no one but Freud had the right to hold this office. In this vein I spoke for almost half-an-hour.

Following me, Adler made a speech sounding the same note. Then it was put to a vote, and a large majority was against the motion. The physicians from Vienna and Germany voted as one man against Ferenczi. (I should mention here that many German psychoanalysts had been won over to the new science by my book on *Anxiety States*.)

After the exciting first session was finished, I invited my Viennese colleagues to a secret meeting. Nearly twenty came, and I lost no time in addressing them. Psychoanalysis, I said, had been founded in Vienna; for a long time we had been the only ones to fight for Freud. It would be preposterous if Vienna were deprived of the leadership. We had to stand for the independence of the new science. Were we to be dependent upon the mercy of Zurich?

Never, they answered. At this moment the door opened; we looked around and saw it was Freud. He was greatly excited, and tried to persuade us to accept Ferenczi's motion; he predicted hard times and a strong opposition by official science. He grasped his coat and

DR. CARL G. JUNG OF ZURICH, SWITZERLAND

cried, "They begrudge me the coat I am wearing; I don't know whether in the future I will earn my daily bread." Tears were streaming down his cheeks. "An official psychiatrist and a Gentile must be the leader of the movement." He foresaw a growing anti-Semitism.

We tried to persuade him that his misgivings were exaggerated. There was a long argument pro and con. Finally he proposed a compromise. We should elect a president to serve for two years, and every two years there should be a new election. We also agreed that there would be no censorship.

We accepted the compromise advocated by our adored master. As a result, at the next session Jung was elected president to serve for two years; but Freud was surprised when I announced that Adler and I were going to found an independent monthly journal devoted to psychoanalysis. The proposed publication was to be known as *Zentralblatt für Psychoanalyse*. The fight with Jung was on. Freud invited us to come to a coffee-house, and there he started the conversation.

"I have written to two publishers concerning the journal. Both are willing to accept our offer if I acknowledge that I am the editor. What kind of a guarantee can you give me that this journal will not be directed against me?"

We stressed the fact that we were his pupils, and that it would be preposterous to assume that we would write against him. Naturally, we reserved the right to propound our own ideas.

Freud suggested a compromise: every paper published had to be censored by us three, Freud, Adler, and

Verlag von J. F. Bergmann in Wiesbaden.

Zentralblatt

für

Psychoanalyse.

Medizinische Monatsschrift für Seelenkunde.

Herausgeber:

Professor Dr. **Sigm. Freud.**

Schriftleitung:

Dr. **Alfred Adler,** Wien. — Dr. **Wilhelm Stekel,** Wien.

Unter Mitwirkung von:

Dr. Karl Abraham, Berlin; Dr. R. G. Assagioli, Florenz; Dr. Ludwig Binswanger, Kreuzlingen; Dr. Poul Bjerre, Stockholm; Dr. A. A. Brill, New-York; Dr. M. Eitingon, Berlin; Dr. D. Epstein, Kiew; Dr. S. Ferenczi, Budapest; Dr. Max Graf, Wien; Dr. Magnus Hirschfeld, Berlin; Dr E. Hitschmann, Wien; Dr. E. Jones, Toronto; Dr. Otto Juliusburger, Steglitz; Dozent C. G. Jung, Zürich; Dr. F. S. Krauss, Wien; Professor August v. Luzenberger, Neapel; Prof. Gustav Modena, Ancona; Dr. Alfons Mäder, Zürich; Dr. Richard Nepalleck, Wien; Dozent N. Ossipow, Moskau; Dr. Oskar Pfister, Zürich; Dr. James Putnam, Boston; Otto Rank, Wien; Dr. R. Reitler, Wien; Dr. Franz Riklin, Zürich; Dr. I. Sadger, Wien; Dr. L. Seif, München; Dr. A. Stegmann, Dresden; Dr. M. Wulff, Odessa; Dr. Erich Wulffen, Dresden.

Jährlich erscheinen 12 Hefte im Gesamt-Umfang von 36–40 Druckbogen zum Jahrespreise von 15 Mark.

FIRST ISSUE OF THE *Zentralblatt für Psychoanalyse*

Stekel. Any of these three had the right to veto the publication of a paper. We accepted. The first issue of the journal came out. Freud was editor-in-chief, Adler and myself were assistant editors. There was a paper by Freud on "Wild Analysis," and there were articles by Adler and myself. We had enough subscribers, and the journal was continued until World War I. All copies were sold out, and second-hand volumes commanded good prices.

I must mention a curious episode. Freud directed the first veto against me; it concerned an essay entitled *The Obligation of the Name*. I proved by many examples that the name very often determines the bearer's whole life, and is especially important for the choice of his vocation. Freud anticipated that people would sneer at me, and in conformity with our agreement he exercised his first objection. I then published the paper in another psychological journal. There was neither sneering nor ridicule; on the contrary, confirmation came from most ardent Freudians.

It is interesting how I obtained knowledge of this phenomenon. I was analyzing a patient who suffered from morbid doubt. In his place of business he had to sort and prepare for mailing some few packages out of hundreds. "I have the compulsion to count these packages again and again, and I am never sure."

"What's your last name?"

"Sure. . . ."

There were many similar examples; later Abraham and Silberer confirmed this phenomenon by many observations of their own.

THE VIENNA CIRCLE

The Vienna Circle now constituted a club. Adler became the president, and I was the vice-president. In addition, many prominent scientists acted as chairmen, including Freud, himself.

I advised Adler to write a book on *The Nervous Character* and recommended him to my publisher.[1] My book on dreams was published in 1911. I had discovered many dream symbols and explained the symbolism of death in several chapters. One evening was set aside in our group for the discussion of this book. I did not expect acknowledgment, for I had already suffered bitter disappointments. Many times I had spoken about "mental bipolarity," and proved that our affects are bipolar. Desire and disgust, love and hate, will-to-power and will-to-submission, are composed of negative and positive parts like the current of electricity. My contention was that any human affect has its own counterpart. Later Bleuler described this fact as "ambivalence," a term that was accepted by everybody, whereas previously they had laughed at my discovery, and had given me the nickname "Stekel with his Bipolarity."

The discussion of my work proved even more unfavorable than I had feared. Among the new members was a very gifted physician named Tausk, a former judge, who for some unknown reason was an especially severe critic of mine. Every new member of the club had to deliver a maiden speech. Tausk had spoken on "Philosophy and Psychoanalysis," promising to build a bridge

---

[1] *Über den Nervösen Character*, Verl. J. F. Bergmann, Wiesbaden, 1912.

between the philosophers and Freud. He had started off excellently, but in the middle of the speech he became confused and was unable to finish. It was an uncomfortable moment for all. I tried to save the situation and continued the lecture extemporaneously. Perhaps he had never forgiven me; at the next opportunity he decried my new book, and spoke at length about the mistakes in grammar in the preface. Every sentence was minutely scrutinized. I have never studied grammar carefully, and I write so fast that sometimes mistakes in grammar do occur. Somerset Maugham in his book, *The Summing Up,* mentions that a secretary found an enormous number of mistakes in the manuscript of one of his novels. He asked a grammatical pundit whether she was right, and was astonished to learn that she was.

The subsequent speakers all belittled my book. Many spoke only about the preface. I expected acknowledgment from Freud, but even he failed me. The only exception was Adler who, at that time, was my friend.

I had the last word. "Mr. Chairman and Gentlemen: An architect built a new house; he was very proud of the arrangement of the rooms, the corridors. He was proud of the facade, of various improvements. He believed that the house was his masterpiece. He invited his colleagues to inspect the house, and was eager to listen to their opinion. The first colleague noticed that the lavatory was not big enough, the second repeated the same criticism, and so on to the last. 'But gentlemen,' cried the desperate architect, 'the daring staircase, the arrangement of the rooms, every room well-lit, the facade—.' But all they spoke about was the lavatory. My dear colleagues, haven't I the same fate? I will do my best to

improve the lavatory; and thank you for your criticism."
Thereupon, I left the room.

My book has been studied by many psychotherapists
in many lands as a textbook of dream symbolism. Freud,
who had not uttered one word of praise during the
critical meeting, later accepted many of my findings.[2]
He confessed to me once (in a "weak" moment) that
every new conception offered by others finds him re-
sistant and unreceptive. Sometimes he required two
weeks to overcome such resistance.

ANXIETY

As stated above, my first difference with Freud began
after my discovery that anxiety states are curable by
psychotherapy. Freud made his great discoveries from
his study of hysteria. He believed at that time that
anxiety neuroses and phobias were organic diseases and
that, therefore, they could not be influenced by psychoanalysis. Fate brought me a patient who proved that
even anxiety states may be caused by a psychic conflict,
and that these are curable if you are able to find a solution for the mental cleavage. Let me return to this
patient. He was a cashier in a big bank, and had held this
position for some time; he could not cross a square.
When he tried to do so, he experienced an intense

---

[2] *Ges. Schriften* (Coll. Papers) , Vol. III: Examination dreams (p. 50) ,
mixed symbols (p. 56) , dream in the dream (p. 63) , "typical symbols"
(p. 66) , genital symbols (p. 73) , right and left, and death symbolism
(p. 74) , numeral symbolism (p. 75) , excretory dreams (p. 76) , and in
other places of this and other volumes.—*The Editor.*

anxiety, his whole body trembled and he had to go to his destination by some roundabout way.

It did not help when someone accompanied him. In my practice I had contended with several cases of agoraphobia. Like a lightning flash it came to my mind: You must discover a psychic cause for this strange illness. According to Freud's rule, I asked about the patient's sex life and about masturbation. Everything was normal. The man had never fallen in love. That aroused my suspicion. A man of twenty-seven, and he had never been in love with a girl. There must be some family fixation. I asked about his family, about home conditions, and finally the following facts came out. His very good mother suffered from cholecystitis. The physician recommended that she go to Carlsbad, but the trip would cost too much, and my patient was in financial distress.

I had a flash of intuition.

"Does much money go through your hands?"

"Hundreds of thousands of *guldens*."

"Have you never thought that if you ran away with this money you could save your mother's life?"

The patient blushed and stammered. "The thought did not come into my mind. It was immediately rejected. I am an honest man and have no inclination toward becoming a criminal."

Now I explained to him that in front of the public square which he could not cross he was playing with the fancy that he had committed a fraud and had to cross the ocean and, at the same time, he had to prove to himself that such a thing would never happen. The square was the symbol of the ocean; "this side" represented Europe, "the other side" America. His phobia was a means of self-defense against his unconscious criminal impulse.

The cashier asked: "What can I do?"

"Give up your post as cashier."

"How can I do that? How shall I explain that I am giving up a job which is only entrusted to men of great integrity?"

"I will give you a certificate to the effect that the responsibility makes you nervous."

"All right," he rejoined.

After a year he sent his sister to me for treatment. She told me he had been transferred to another branch of the bank and that his agoraphobia had disappeared.

The second case was a little more dramatic. One morning I was called to a family for a consultation. I was led into a room where I found a young, voluptuous-looking woman holding the hands of a weakly built man. The man cried, "You see how unhappy I am. I have to be at the office at nine o'clock and my wife keeps me as a prisoner, because if I leave her she has a fit of panic. This is the worst fit she has ever had." He told me the story. "The disease started a year ago. First she could not walk alone. She had to be accompanied, usually by a member of her family, later by two members of my family, and now I am the only one who can protect her against her panic. Lately she has had attacks even in the room."

I calmed the lady down, and the husband asked me to come into another room. There he made the striking confession that he had been married for seven years, but his wife was still a virgin. Again my intuition helped me: She is protecting herself against temptation! When her cravings for satisfaction increase, it is only her husband who can defend her against the danger of yielding to them. The only treatment that can help her is to cure her husband of impotence. This I did.

A third case sent to me by Freud revealed the same psychological root.

In his first papers Freud described the anxiety neurosis as a consequence of an abnormal sex behavior. He did not know anything about the psychic substratum of this disease. He believed, for instance, that the damage done by masturbation led to neurasthenia.

I claim it as a merit to have first recognized that this whole branch of neurosis was psychically determined, and that nothing but psychotherapy would relieve or cure it.

I was proud to explain to Freud the psychic mechanism underlying these cases. He was astounded, and said: "But such cases are not 'anxiety neuroses.' They are without exception cases of hysteria."

Freud knew that I wanted to report these cases in my book on *Nervous Anxiety*. He asked me to come the next day, and received me with the words, "I will give you a royal present; we shall call all cases where the anxiety has a psychological root, 'anxiety hysteria,' while cases where anxiety can be traced to injuries of the sex life will be called 'anxiety neurosis.'"

In the second edition of my book on *Anxiety States*, I renounced Freud's control and corrected some of his errors, especially his opinion that masturbation leads to neurasthenia. I also declared that variations of the sexual life which Freud found harmful (such as coitus interruptus) are never the cause of an anxiety neurosis. I had expressed this view in 1907 in an article on *Nervous Anxiety States* which appeared in the "Medizinische Klinik" in Vienna, and also in my pamphlet on *Causes of Nervousness*[3] which was published at about the same time. I have remained faithful to this formulation ever since: *Every neurosis is the result of a mental conflict.* Freud later adopted some of my discoveries without mentioning my name. Even the fact that in my first edition I had defined anxiety as the reaction of the *life instinct* against the upsurge of the *death instinct* was not mentioned in his later books,[4] and many people believe that the death instinct is Freud's discovery.

Freud never changed his views regarding the somatic origin of neuroses. In his brilliant autobiography[5] he still deals with the term "actual neurosis" (anxiety neurosis and neurasthenia) and distinguishes this somatogenic (sexo-toxic) neurosis from "psychoneurosis" (hysteria and compulsion neurosis). In his autobiography he says as follows:

Thus I was led to recognize neuroses in general as disturbances of the sexual function; the so-called "actual neuroses" as a direct toxic expression of these disturbances and the "psychoneuroses" as their psychic expression. My medical conscience felt gratified by this arrangement. I hoped that I had filled a gap in medical science which was hitherto willing to accept no other injuries to that biologically so important function than those incurred by infection or gross anatomic lesion. The

3 "Ursachen der Nervositaet," Paul Knepler, Vienna, 1907.
4 *Jenseits des Lustprinzips*, Int. Psa. Verlag, 1920. English edition, *Beyond the Pleasure Principle*, (Liveright Publishing Corp., 1949).
5 "Die Medizin der Gegenwart in Selbstdarstellungen," Vol. IV. Felix Meixer, Leipzig, 1925.

*medical concept benefited also from the fact that sex
was not only a psychic matter. It had also a somatic side,
one could ascribe to it a specific chemism, and could
trace the sexual stimulation to the presence of specific
(though as yet unknown) matter. It must also have had
a special reason that genuine spontaneous neuroses show
resemblance to no other group of diseases more than
with the manifestations of intoxication and abstinence
seen following the introduction or withdrawal of certain
toxic matter, or with Graves' disease, whose dependency
on a product of the thyroid gland is well known.*

*I had later no more opportunity to resume my investi-
gations on actual neuroses. Neither was this part of my
work continued by others. . . .*

What does that mean? The actual neurosis still exists,
but Freud has no opportunity to investigate it, or it has
become less important. A similar statement can be found
in his book on *Inhibition, Symptom, and Anxiety*[6] regarding the question whether libido can be transformed
directly into anxiety. He says there (page 105, Ges. Schr.
Vol. XI) : "The formerly maintained direct transformation of libido into anxiety has now become less important to us (". . . *ist unserem Interesse nun weniger
bedeutsam geworden"*) .

ADLER'S SECESSION

Meanwhile, an important change in the club was in
the making. Adler went his own way and was working
on a theory which was different from that of Freud. He
was intuitive and full of new ideas, but at first tried to

---

[6] Int. Psa. Verlag, Vienna, 1926.

Zentralblatt

für

Psychoanalyse.

Medizinische Monatsschrift für Seelenkunde.

Organ der Internationalen Psychoanalytischen Vereinigung.

Herausgeber: Prof. Dr. Sigm. Freud.

Schriftleiter: Dr. Wilhelm Stekel, Wien, Gonzagagasse 21.

Unter Mitwirkung von:

Dr. Karl Abraham, Berlin; Dr. R. G. Assagioli, Florenz; Dr. Ludwig Binswanger, Kreuzlingen; Dr. Poul Bjerre, Stockholm; Dr. A. A. Brill, New-York; Dr. M. Eitingon, Berlin; Dr. D. Epstein, Kiew; Dr. S. Ferenczi, Budapest; Dr. Max Graf, Wien; Dr. Magnus Hirschfeld, Berlin; Dr. E. Hitschmann, Wien; Professor E. Jones, Toronto; Dr. Otto Juliusburger, Steglitz; Dozent C. G. Jung, Zürich; Dr. F. S. Krauss, Wien; Professor August v. Luzenberger, Neapel; Prof. Gustav Modena, Ancona; Dr. Alfons Mäder, Zürich; Dr. Richard Nepalleck, Wien; Dozent N. Ossipow, Moskau; Dr. Oskar Pfister, Zürich; Dr. James Putnam, Boston; Otto Rank, Wien; Dr. R. Reitler, Wien; Dr. Franz Riklin, Zürich; Dr. J. Sadger, Wien; Dr. L. Seif, München; Dr. A. Stegmann, Dresden; Dr. M. Wulff, Odessa; Dr. Erich Wulffen, Dresden.

II. Jahrgang Heft 3.

Dezember.

Wiesbaden.

Verlag von J. F. Bergmann.

1911.

40 Jährlich erscheinen 12 Hefte im Gesamt-Umfang von 36 bis Druckbogen zum Jahrespreise von 18 Mark.

Zentralblatt für Psychoanalyse FOR DECEMBER, 1911

adapt his theory to Freud's. Freud invited him to give several lectures on his research, as we all wished to know more about it in order to do him full justice. Adler was highly pleased. Once while walking with me he said, "What's the matter with Freud? Is he really willing to compromise with me and to accept my deviations? What's his game?" Adler prepared himself very carefully for his talks, and in the three following sessions gave a clear exposition of his psychology (now called "Individual Psychology"). The fourth week was reserved for the discussion. I was not prepared for what followed. One Freudian after another got up and denounced, in well-prepared speeches, the new concepts of Adler. Even Freud himself read a paper against his pupil. The atmosphere was very tense, but the excitement reached its peak when one of the members, Max Steiner, a faithful shield-bearer of Freud's, pointed out that Adler's theories were so different from the views of our master that one might question Adler's justification in being a member of our circle. Steiner's remark sounded like a motion. I argued that we should attempt to find the common denominator in the different theories. It would be ridiculous to believe that any deviation from Freud constituted an act of rebellion. Such an attitude would not be in keeping with the idea of freedom of science. However, the majority was against Adler; thereupon he and eight of his adherents left the room.

Adler at this time was a fanatical socialist, and all his followers were partisans. (Politics often determine scientific convictions!)

Why did I not leave with Adler? I was partly depen-

dent on Freud for my practice and, in addition, I wanted
to wait and see how matters would develop. I stayed with
Freud, and edited our journal with him. Another important motive was that I was so fond of the journal, so
proud of its success, that I did not want to give it up if
I could help it.

At the next meeting, Freud defended his behavior
toward Adler. He said, "Adler isn't a normal man. His
jealousy and ambition are morbid." Later on, in private,
he said to me, "I think Adler's new ideas are worthless.
One of your discoveries in the field of dream symbols
has more value than all these far-fetched philosophical
hypotheses." He tried to favor me in every way; from
Carlsbad he sent me a valuable ashtray and wrote in his
letter: *I don't know what could ever separate us.*

SEPARATION FROM FREUD

But we were soon separated. Perhaps Jung was working against me, and Freud was afraid to lose him. Freud
told me once that he had to defend me against Jung
who maintained that I was a nuisance to psychoanalysis.

At one session my honor was personally attacked by
Victor Tausk. He insinuated that my cases were invented. (If I had invented my cases I should undoubt-
edly be a greater poet than Shakespeare.) During this
speech by Tausk, I wrote to Freud on a scrap of paper,
"If you will not rebuke these personal attacks, this is the
last time that I shall have been a member of this circle."
In a mild manner Freud asked Tausk to avoid personal
remarks.

The next stroke was more serious. I had dedicated my best gifts to our journal. I had been very careful to review all papers and books without prejudice. (Prejudice is the hangman of Truth.) I read and studied, and I wrote many reviews. But one day Freud suggested that all analytical papers should be reviewed in our journal by Tausk. I reminded Freud of our agreement and said that I had the right of veto, but he remained adamant. I gave up my membership in the group. At this time I was president.

I paid my last visit to Freud, and he mentioned again how he had to protect me against the insinuations of Jung. "Dear Master," I said, "I am afraid that in a short time you will see you have sacrificed your most faithful collaborator for an ungrateful one. Jung will not remain a Freudian long."

"Let's hope you are mistaken," answered Freud, sighing.

I was correct as far as Jung was concerned. After a spirited discussion at the next International Congress, Jung separated from Freud and became the founder of his own school (Analytical Psychology). Jung may have been offended because of his jealousy of the success of Freud's fascinating book, *Totem and Taboo,* a field in which Jung had done considerable research. Freud described brilliantly the customs of primitives and found in them the confirmation of some of his basic views regarding mental disorders. Whatever the reason, Jung established his own school and won over many pupils and admirers.

Meanwhile, Freud published a new periodical, *Imago.* It was dedicated to the psychoanalytical illumination of

Zentralblatt

für

Psychoanalyse und Psychotherapie.

Medizinische Monatsschrift für Seelenkunde.

Schriftleiter:

Dr. Wilhelm Stekel, Wien, Gonzagagasse 21.
Vom 15. Juni bis zum 15. September Bad Ischl — Kaltenbachstrasse 26.

III. Jahrgang, Heft 8/9.

Mai/Juni.

Wiesbaden.
Verlag von J. F. Bergmann.
1913.

Jährlich erscheinen 12 Hefte im Gesamt-Umfang von mindestens.
40 Druckbogen zum Jahrespreise von 18 Mark.
Zentralblatt für Psychoanalyse und Psychotherapie
FOR MAY-JUNE, 1913

Dr. Alfred Adler

Art, Science, and Religion. My publisher, Bergmann, protested in vain against this new competition. We were both afraid that we might lose some interesting items for our journal.

After our separation, Freud was confident that he would get the editorship of the *Zentralblatt* for himself and Tausk, but Bermann did not cooperate. I remained the sole editor of the *Zentralblatt*. We lost some subscribers but I enlarged the circle of interest and the journal became a platform for all kinds of psychotherapy. I still believed that in every method there was something useful, and that we should take the good where we find it. I edited the journal for two years until World War I put an end to it.

Chapter Six

PRACTICING PSYCHOANALYSIS

★

PSYCHOSOMATIC DISORDERS

A. BELLADONNA

I HAD ENOUGH private patients. My spare time was reduced to a few hours. Many who came to me were directed to other physicians. But, even with my schedule so full, I treated two new patients, and was fortunate enough to cure them. One was a well-read, emotional and intelligent Hungarian woman who had tried various treatments. The other was a seventeen-year-old baroness who was suffering from nightmares and morbid fears. The baroness, when walking in the street, saw vast numbers of hallucinatory snakes and had to jump over them. I discovered that her pupils were always enlarged and asked her about it. She admitted that she had put drops of an atropine solution into her eyes in order to give them an alluring expression. I knew by experience that belladonna was able to produce mental confusion.

One of the first cases Freud had sent to me was that of a traveling salesman who had fainted one day, revived after ten minutes, but had lost his memory. Freud suspected amnesia. I had heard that this man was troubled with stomach pains, that there was some suspicion of an ulcer, and that he was given belladonna to relieve the pains. One day I chanced to read in a medical paper that belladonna, under certain circumstances, is able to produce amnesia and even a transient mental confusion. I told the family of this man that psychoanalytic treatment would most probably not be necessary, and that the patient would be cured in a short time if he stopped using belladonna. His memory returned after two weeks.

I had a similar success with the young baroness, but I had to go on with the analytical treatment because the nightmares and the phobias did not cease.

B. APHASIA

After my return from Hungary, a young officer entreated me to try my luck with his father. He knew a patient I had cured, and was told that I had shown great patience. My visitor's father had been in a sanatorium for seven months following a stroke; he was too weak to walk; sitting in a wheel chair in the garden, or in his bed, he did not talk except to say, "I can't." He suffered from a postapoplectic aphasia. Whatever you asked him the only answer was, "I can't." I explained to the son that I had no time to attend to such a case but he was willing to compensate me for any loss of time.

I met the impressive old man with clear-cut features and a long white beard in a pleasant sitting room overlooking a garden. He answered my greetings by moving his head. I asked him if he was willing to be treated and got the usual reaction, "I can't." My experience with the schizophrenic sculptress came into my mind[1] and I intended to use the same patience. Are there incurable cases? Let us try, anyhow. So I came every day, talked to the patient in a kindly manner. He looked at me with his big eyes as though he were interested. Except for the stereotyped answer I could not get any reaction. After two weeks of this hopeless procedure, I said to his son, "Let's finish this fruitless treatment. I am wasting my time and you your money." The son insisted that I should go on. He was convinced that his father's real trouble was psychogenic. He would take the responsibility and never blame me if the treatment should prove unsuccessful. I tried the same method I had used in the case of the sculptress. I asked my old patient to stand up and to make some steps in the room with my support. "I can't" was his answer.

"But you must," I said to him with a more severe intonation of my voice. Slowly he stood up. He had an imposing figure, and was very tall. I hardly reached the level of his shoulders. At first he made only a few steps. Then we progressed more and more and finally, we were able to walk into the garden of the sanatorium. The walk was extended to one hour and he could find his balance without being supported. He started to talk to me. I felt ashamed: The son, a layman, understood the case better than the psychoanalyst. I admired the touching love of the officer for his father.

After marked improvement had been achieved, the

---

[1] This case is reported on page 162.—*The Editor.*

patient left the sanatorium and was brought into an elegant apartment in the best hotel of Vienna. Visitors were coming and going, and could not understand the change. The old man walked up and down in front of his hotel for a few hours daily.

What was the cloven hoof behind the behavior of the son? My patient's affairs had been put under trusteeship; the son asked me to call in a well-known neuropsychiatrist for consultation and requested that we should explain in a certificate that the patient was now absolutely normal and able to come to legally valid decisions. The consultant arrived, examined the patient for more than an hour, and wrote a certificate to the effect that the invalid was now mentally recovered and in full control of his intellectual powers. Next day the officer explained his plans to me. In the last will of his very rich father he did not get his fair share. He knew my great influence upon his father. I was to suggest to the old gentleman that he should make a new will; he hoped his father would be grateful to the son who was instrumental in his recovery.

Now I found the solution of the riddle. It was not the touching love of a child, it was the cupidity of a would-be heir.

Other members of the family, favored by the last will, seemed to have guessed the intention of the son. They were afraid lest a new will be drawn and implored me to prevent such an unjustified step. They even wanted me to call in new authorities in order to prove that their father was not totally recovered. It was an ugly affair. I stopped the visits to my patient. By accident, I got rid of the frequent visits of the son. Some time later he was transferred to front duty and was killed by shrapnel. My patient relapsed more and more into his former state and was finally taken back to the sanatorium. His speech again became restricted to the words "I can't." Later, I understood those words: I was informed that before the stroke his son had asked him to make a new will. Did the emotion induced by the request cause the stroke? I was told that after a while my patient could speak a few words, but he suffered a new stroke and died a few months later.

Was this an exceptional case or are there similar cases? There is only one rule: never lose patience! Some cases demand a difficult sacrifice of time, and then amply reward the devotion of the physician with unexpected success. Many patients are cured because someone is interested in their cases. Often, it is not the method that is responsible for the success, it is the satisfaction of the patient's desire for sympathy, of his longing for interest and companionship. This fact may explain the success of different schools of psychotherapy; it shows that success can never prove a method to be "right."

C. STRABISMUS

I had the opportunity to treat a particularly interesting case of psychogenic strabismus. The patient was an American lawyer who suffered from various neurotic symptoms. The outstanding one was his squint; his eyes wandered to right and left and it was difficult for him to read. He had to study long briefs and to read books but in spite of his thick glasses he usually had to stop reading after a few minutes. In addition to this, he could not wear stiff collars; he invariably wore his shirt open at the throat, and had the peculiar tic of running his fingers round his collar as though he wanted to have more air for breathing. He was hard-up because he had married against the wish of his rich mother. She did not give the couple any financial support. He worked in a friend's office and earned a small salary; it was difficult for him to make ends meet.

He brought me a dream which he had submitted to different analysts in the hope of getting the right interpretation. The dream was as follows:

I was in a law-court accused of having killed my mother. The lawyer defended me by mentioning the fact that my mother was still alive. There was a long discussion as to whether it was possible for a dead person to be still alive. This discussion went on for hours, and I lost my patience. I looked at the court, at the judges, and said: You may kiss my a—, and left the court.

First the story and then my interpretation. Before his marriage, the patient was a gay Lothario. He passed like a bee from one flower to another. A sociable, burly fellow, it was not difficult for him to make conquests. But one girl, the most attractive he had ever met, resisted for a long time. He wrote her many love letters and went so far as to promise her marriage. On these terms she gave herself to him before marriage. After a while she became pregnant and he was compelled to marry her. The girl had kept his letters and he was at her mercy. It was during the war, and he had to go to France as an officer. He married her without his mother's knowledge and sailed for Europe. The infant, a girl, was born while he was abroad.

He stayed in France for two years. Though he was a sensual man, he was absolutely continent; being extremely jealous, he was afraid of retaliation in kind. He returned to his wife and daughter in America. Though he was intensely passionate, his marriage turned out to be an unhappy one because of his morbid jealousy. It was an ordeal for both his wife and him to walk together on the street. She was not allowed to look to the right or to the left, and any man who greeted her was suspected of being a secret lover. The home turned into an inferno; quarrels and reproaches were followed by reconciliation, and—usually—by passionate intercourse.

I asked the patient for the associations to the dream. The only association he was able to produce was the fact that the lawyer in the dream was the same one who had defended a man who had killed his wife with a hatchet. The man was later hanged for this crime.

I explained the dream to him as follows: "You haven't killed your mother, but you have killed your love for your mother, and her love for you. Your relationship with your mother is finished. Besides, you have criminal impulses to kill your wife and to become reconciled with your mother, but you are afraid of being hanged for the crime. That is why you cannot wear a stiff collar, and the way you play with your collar comes from the feeling that you already have the rope around your neck."

"And what about my eye trouble?"

"There are various reasons for that. First, you are

mentally blind to your problems. You do not want to see the truth; you do not want to know what is going on in your mind. The most important fact is that you have forbidden your wife to look to the right or to the left in the street. When walking in the street you are determined to look straight ahead, and not to see the pretty girls passing right and left. (At that time it was the fashion to wear short skirts, and girls freely exposed their more or less pretty calves.) Against your conscious will your eyes are swerving to the right and to the left, so that you can—unwillingly—see the girls around you. This behavior is in keeping with your polygamous nature and your past as a Don Juan. All the time you are pretending (to yourself) that you are looking straight ahead."

The effect of this interpretation was remarkable. The patient came to the next session wearing a stiff collar and without his thick glasses. He was able to read with ease and he felt like a new-born man. (The consequence of this success was that a great many near-sighted and far-sighted people came to me during the next few weeks, believing that I was an exceptionally able ophthalmologist.)

D. HYPOGLYCAEMIA

In many diseases you will find a mixture of psychic and organic factors. One of my patients had a spell of depression. I visited him in his boarding house. He was so weak that he could not get up. He looked haggard, and I was told that during the whole day he had taken no other food than a cup of tea without sugar. At this

moment I suspected he was suffering from hypoglycaemia. I remembered that he was very fond of sweets,
always had some chocolates in his pocket, and ate them
at intervals during the analysis. I ordered a test to determine the amount of sugar in his blood. The sugar
tolerance test confirmed my supposition. I asked the
patient to drink a strong solution of sugar. In a short
time he was a different being: his cheeks grew rosy, his
pulse calmed down, he felt strong again, and he left his
bed looking like a new man.

E. AEROPHAGIA

I have frequently observed that some patients use
tricks to increase their psychic troubles. A man who suffered from anxiety states told me that when he had to
cross the streets, he sighed, breathed deeply and frequently, and swallowed air. The distended stomach
pressed on the diaphragm, the diaphragm pressed on
the heart; the attacks of palpitation were partly due to
excitement, partly to aerophagia. Here we have a vicious
circle in which one symptom increases the other.

F. THE QUINCKE EDEMA

What is science? It is the recognition of a new truth,
not the defense of an ancient dogma. In this connection,
let me recount a most instructive episode.

I once treated a case of Quincke's disease (angio-
neurotic edema). The patient was a lady, aged forty,
who suffered at intervals from extremely disfiguring at-

tacks of edematous urticaria of the face and hands. For seven years she had been ineffectually treated at various clinics. One of her doctors recognized the malady was psychogenic, and for that reason sent her to me. I handed her over to my Dutch pupil, Lingbeck, who discovered the following facts: The patient, a married woman with an adult daughter, secured adequate sexual gratification with a lover but not with her husband. The attacks of angio-neurotic edema always seized her after a visit to the lover, and were obviously a self-inflicted punishment for infidelity. (Fear lest the daughter might learn of the mother's misconduct was also contributory.) We advised her to discontinue the extramarital relations. She heeded our words and the attacks of Quincke's disease ceased.

At my insistence, Dr. Lingbeck brought the case to the notice of the Medical Society. Our observations invalidated the hitherto existing opinion that an adequate sexual gratification is a cure for neurotic disorders. Here the neurotic symptoms followed adequate sexual gratification, but ceased when the gratification was renounced. When this had been explained, one of the doctors voiced his objection: the case presentation was not suitable for the Medical Society. The results had been due to chance, he contended, and had nothing to do with science. This declaration was vociferously applauded.

I intervened with the statement that time would show whether the inference of Lingbeck and myself had or had not been "scientific."

The patient was seated in the ante-room listening to the rather heated discussion. Her natural reaction was:

"These experts do not believe that my malady was caused by my love affair. Why, then, should I deprive myself?" That very day she phoned to her lover; they made an appointment, and she enjoyed herself in the old way. But within a few hours she had a distressing attack of Quincke edema, and came ruefully to consult Lingbeck. He and I were able to convince her that the illness was a conscience reaction. Now she permanently broke off the liaison, and was permanently cured. As to the last statement I was reassured when I again saw her several years afterwards.

G. EPILEPSY

Meanwhile I had made a discovery of high importance. I treated cases of epilepsy, was often surprisingly successful, and I learned by experience that many cases of so-called epilepsy are mentally conditioned, or are complicated by a psychic superstructure. In many cases you may improve the condition of patients, in some you may cure them completely. My desire was to drag the patient out of his isolation and idleness, and to induce him to work. Even if he continued to have fits, they were, in any case, diminished in number. I was able to make him a useful member of society.

After the publication of my paper on epilepsy, I was sent an issue of a journal, *Der Wendepunkt* ("The Turning Point"), edited by the Swiss physician, Dr. Bircher-Benner, a pioneer in dietetics. The leading article in this issue called "A Great Triumph in Science" gave a summary of my research on epilepsy. I was pleased because it was the only affirmative voice among views that were otherwise invariably unfavorable. Clinicians treated me as a "fantastic mind," and were far from acknowledging that I worked hard to bring light into a dark problem of medicine. Like a lioness defending her cub, so the psychiatrists defended epilepsy as an incurable organic disease.

(Bircher-Benner was enthusiastic about the fact that in my psychic treatment the use of narcotics was barred. I found that narcotics reduce the activity of the patient and bring about regression into day-dreaming. The epileptic finally becomes a drug-addict.)

I once treated a patient suffering from what was described as "genuine epilepsy." Surgical operation had been fruitlessly tried, but psychotherapy was successful. Did this "prove" anything? No, for doctors insisted that if the patient was cured, the diagnosis of "genuine epilepsy" must have been wrong. My view that some cases of "genuine epilepsy" are psychogenic was dismissed as "unscientific."

WAR PSYCHIATRY

During the first World War, I was working at the neuro-psychiatric section of a large war hospital in Vienna. It was built for three thousand patients. My department had two barracks with a hundred and forty patients, all told; besides this, I was busy with consultations from other departments. By a strange coincidence, Alfred Adler was my predecessor. He had been transferred to a provincial town, although he had done excellent work here. His examinations were profound, his histories of the diseases were blameless, he was a model physician.

I did not know that I obtained this responsible position only on trial. The first cases, with my findings and diagnoses, were sent without my knowledge to be perused by some prominent men. I had good luck. I was very cautious. Every new patient had to undergo a thorough examination. In my first three cases, I had to decide between a serious organic disease and malingering; my diagnoses were confirmed. In a short time I enjoyed the confidence of all my colleagues and later I was given the right of independent decision; my decisions were accepted without further supervision.

I sympathized with the poor soldiers, and tried to protect them as much as possible. This became known among them and they felt confident of my good will. Even malingerers confessed. I despised those physicians who, as slave-drivers for the war-mongers, forced half-recovered soldiers to go back to the trenches. I have seen terrible examples of the work of these executioners. Convalescents, still in pain, their wounds unhealed, were marched off to their regiments. In many hospitals they were tortured with a faradic brush, so that they preferred the terrors of war to the terrors of the hospital. Every week, the chief of the hospital, a major and former dentist, came into the ward and shouted, "We must evacuate! Send fifty per cent of the patients away! A new transport is coming!" At the same time, disgraceful favoritism existed in the hospital. The chief, the head-nurse, and two sergeants formed a corrupt clique. Rich patients loafed for months and months. In order to keep them in the hospital, they were classified as suffering from non-existent diseases. Often I had to fight to protect the soldiers against undue cruelty. The whole corruption was covered with a superficial varnish of hypocritical religion: every Sunday all physicians had to go to mass. It was the wish of the almighty pious headnurse. In the first row sat the Major in his best attire. He was puffed up with self-righteousness.

Some cases I would have liked to analyze. There were so many shell-shocked soldiers, hysterics, tremblers, dancers, the paralyzed, and the deafened and dumbed. It was as if a sorcerer had transferred me back to the clinic where I studied with Krafft-Ebing. I am convinced that all cases of shell-shock and war hysteria are caused by a psychic conflict; on the one side it is fear of death and disablement, on the other the duty toward the country.

In our hospital, because of lack of time, mental treatment other than hypnosis was impossible. So I started to hypnotize my patients and achieved good results. In my barracks an atmosphere gradually developed that was favorable to hypnosis. These simple people believed I was working with magic. As is known, it is difficult to hypnotize individual neurotics in the office, but it is easy to hypnotize a group of people simultaneously. One is impressed by the example of the other. Therefore, men working with hypnosis often have several particularly submissive patients on whom they perform their miracles before starting with the new patients. Public hypnotists generally have one or two bogus "mediums" (assistants) to implant the suggestion upon others.

I was able to hypnotize most of my patients. Sometimes when I was making my rounds I would achieve a general sedative effect by commanding, "Sleep one hour!" while pointing with my index finger at the individual patient, and one after the other would fall asleep and remain quiet for the required time. Of great help was the fact that I was considered by my patients as their friend and protector—I did not send them back to the trenches until they had recovered. In most cases they were qualified for light service in the "hinterland." During my therapy I often had an audience of other physicians, and the head-nurse never missed my hypnotic sessions.

Among my patients there was a man who had lost his speech following a persistent artillery barrage. I promised to cure him in a few minutes. All the doctors of the hospital together with the chief surgeon and the head-nurse gathered to witness this demonstration. I used a different method—fascination. The patient, a simple Hungarian peasant (I could not communicate with him as I do not speak Hungarian), was sitting opposite me in a chair. I looked persistently into his eyes for two minutes and then I intoned "A-a-a." Like an automaton he repeated the "A." Then I used other vowels, progressed to syllables, and finally he repeated a few Hungarian words I had learned at the hospital. At last the expected miracle occurred: he was cured. A stream of tears broke from his eyes. Was he a malingerer? And did he feel sorry that I had overpowered him? I do not know. I kept him in the hospital for a few weeks and then sent him back to be assigned to light duty.

A CASE OF SCHIZOPHRENIA

A short time before the war began, I was treating a young girl, a mental case. The day I was called to see her, she had smashed all the furniture in her room. Her father told me the story of her disease. In a normal state she had made a trip to Italy. She came back with a slight depression, and in a short time she was so completely unbalanced that her father asked the opinion of the famous psychiatrist, Wagner von Jauregg. He took her into his clinic, but there she became progressively worse. Finally Wagner-Jauregg diagnosed the case as schizophrenia and declared the patient incurable.

I found this beautiful girl, who looked like a doll, in her room in a negativistic state. She did not talk, did not change her dress, and she left her room only for necessities. I spoke to her kindly. She did not answer. I did not lose patience, however. I visited her every day as I tried to establish a contact. She was a sculptress and some of her work was on the table. I spoke about her drawings, sometimes holding her hand, which she permitted without protest. After a week she spoke the first words to her parents. "Why didn't you bring this man sooner?" Nothing else. I knew that I had won the battle. I continued my visits, but she remained mute. For three months she had not left her apartment. After I had seen her for two weeks, I felt I must break her resistance and I followed my intuition; I said to her, "Elizabeth, please put on your coat and let's go for a walk." She looked at me in astonishment, but like an automaton, went to her wardrobe, put on a coat, looked in the mirror for the

first time, combed her hair, and went out with me. She
led me to the studio she shared with another sculptor,
and there she let me see her own work. It was hyper-
modern, but it betrayed much talent. I spoke about her
sculptures and—surprisingly—she responded; thus we
got into a fairly normal conversation.

The resistance was broken, she told me her story and
her dreams, dreams in which often the Holy Virgin
and other religious symbols appeared with symbols of
guilt. It was as though she were soiled. In many dreams
she tried to wash herself; once *she met Lady Macbeth,
who said to her, "All the perfumes of Arabia will not
sweeten this little hand!"* I asked her why she felt so
guilty and she finally told me the story of her trip to
Italy. She had pretended that, accompanied by a friend,
she had made this journey in order to see the beautiful
places and famous pictures. But on the trip she met the
sculptor with whom she shared the studio; and that she
became his mistress. Unfortunately, she had no adequate
sexual gratification that could have served as a compensation for the sacrifice of her virginity.

My conclusion was that she was frigid as a consequence of her religious upbringing. I had seen other
patients, girls and women, who were frigid during their
relations before marriage, but became normal after
marrying the same man. The inhibitions of conscience
were removed by the legalization of the relationship. I
thought marriage with the sculptor would cure this
lady. (Very often it is the other way around: a woman
who has been frigid in marriage becomes passionate in
an illicit union.) I invited the sculptor to see me, explained to him that he was morally responsible for

Elizabeth's disease, and expressed the idea that perhaps marriage would effect a cure. He seemed willing. I hoped that my information concerning her lover's willingness to marry her would have a beneficial influence on my patient's frigidity. But to my astonishment, she reacted in a very different way. "I shall never marry that man," she said. "I don't want to see him again."

The case proved more complicated than I thought. The patient had a very attractive sister, tall and fairhaired. This sister had first conceived the idea of calling me in, and came frequently to the hospital to talk about Elizabeth, who was the pride of the family. I was very fond of the sister and at one time even believed I was in love with her. I wrote a poem (published in my book, *The Wise and the Fool*).[1]

I did not know there was a rivalry between the two sisters as a consequence of a homosexual fixation. (I call that the *tertium quid* of love.) The sculptor had originally been in love with the sister, and Elizabeth "annexed him" to outrival her sister. Had she noticed that I too was interested in her sister? Did she play the same trick on me? Anyway, it was clear that the sister was interested in me, and that our unexpressed affection was mutual.

I did not press further the desirability of marriage between my patient and the sculptor, and he, on his part, was glad to be relieved from the obligation. Meanwhile Elizabeth improved; she gradually became more or less normal and she wrote the story of her "miracu-

---

[1] *Der Weise und der Tor*, published by Paul Knepler, Vienna, 1918.
"Fools they that die for some dead past, in vain!
All he once lost, the Wise man wins again. . . ."

lous cure" in the rich style found only in true poets. But there were still various symptoms left. She would go out only with me or with her father, never alone; she would quarrel with the members of her family; and she had no inclination to resume her former work, her sculpture.

ON A BICYCLE THROUGH THE ALPS

It was the first year of the war. I had been treating maimed and mutilated soldiers. Every day a transport had arrived. The stench of wounded, the dying, and the dead, was sickening. Soldiers came from the front where they had not washed for months, with wounds from which pus oozed, and with frames which were shockingly lacerated. I could not then foresee that after such an experience I was to endure a second "Great War." All these men were innocent victims of war. I asked many soldiers if they knew why there was a war. (My knowledge of different languages was of much help to me.) Most of the wounded men had no definite answer. Others maintained that the Czar wanted to take a part of Austria-Hungary. Later I read the German translation of a Polish novel by Joseph Wittlin, *The Salt of the Earth*. Everybody should read this book. The chief figure in it is a poor Polish peasant, an employee at a little railway station who had to join the army and did not understand why he had to fight or what was happening around him.

I welcomed a fortnight's leave from the horrible environment of the hospital. I decided to satisfy a precious, long-considered desire. I would make a trip by bicycle through the Alps with Eric, my son. The first stop was at the cottage of my patient, Elizabeth. My reception was enthusiastic. I saw that Elizabeth had made considerable progress. She had retained and strengthened her gains, but she still had no inclination for work, was easily depressed, and she quarrelled continuously with her sister.

My cycling tour through the Alps was an enduring joy. Every hour brought us new landscapes, new quaint and quiet places, peaceful little inns; we climbed the mountains and swam in rivers and lakes. There were few cars on the roads. We did not feel tired, even after a whole day's trip. Like a manic excitement! I thought how disappointing sobriety would be after intoxication. It was the warning voice of doubt; but these misgivings were of short duration, and were easily dispelled by the enchantment of the trip. Eric has often told me that this fortnight was the most memorable one in his life, and that he doubts if he will ever again have such an enjoyable experience.

THE VITAMIN OF LOVE

In this phase of my life a second example taught me how love influences creative art. I was called in to see a woman artist who wished to know me personally after she had read some of my books. Her name was familiar to me because I had attended an exhibition of her pictures, which were a sensation at the time. We became friends and she confided her story to me. She said that one day she discovered that her husband was having relations with her servant. She threw a cup of coffee at him and her relations with him ended then and there. Her husband's brother, a young officer, sympathized with her, consoled her, and finally they became attracted to each other. Whereas prior to the incident with her husband she had earned a mediocre livelihood by making copies of paintings and by designing post cards, under the influence of the young officer she commenced to work on her own creations, and soon became famous. However, she couldn't work unless her brother-in-law was in the room. While she was painting, he would invariably read to her, poems or other romantic literature, but she had to hear his voice all the time she was working. It was as if his voice were whispering, "I am here! I am here! And you know I love you!" Even when she was painting a portrait, he was there, reading. Her creations were a compensation for her own lack of beauty in face and form. Her desire for beauty found a medium for expression in her creations. At the beginning of the war she followed her lover to various places and produced some vivid war pictures. But the war separated them. He found another woman. The artist was forsaken. Her power for creative work dwindled, and she went back to doing "copy" work. Her brush had been made effective only by love. Through gratified love she became an artist and overcame her sense of inferiority. Deprived of love, she again became a mere copyist, an undesirable, elderly woman.

DISORDERS OF THE INSTINCTS AND EMOTIONS

My real satisfaction was my work. I had just completed the volume on *Onanie und Homosexualität*, a book which was designed to dispel some of the worst prejudices regarding sex life. It offered scientific proof that the hitherto existing views on abstinence were a fallacy.

While it is certain that social movements are set in action by prevailing social conditions, I am convinced that the individual as such is driven by purely individual motives. I once knew a physician who strongly advocated sexual abstinence. He founded a society for the prevention of venereal disease by sexual abstinence. I found out that whenever this physician attempted to have intercourse with a prostitute he was impotent. What was more logical for him, therefore, than to preach against prostitutes? He transferred his personal conflict to a social issue. Once after a successful speech before his Society a secret thought occurred to him "Tonight I might also be successful with a prostitute." No quicker thought than done. After the meeting he went to a brothel. But, alas! He was again impotent. It is not impossible that after a successful coitus his views might have changed radically.

What conclusions can we draw from the above with regard to our subject? So many books have been written about masturbation and there are so many scientists who are in favor of suppressing it. Are these actions not also safeguards for the individual personality, displacements of personal problems onto social issues? I have stated it repeatedly. Everybody at one time or another has fought a more or less bitter struggle against masturbation which was thought of as a way of shortening one's life. For this reason, the numerous books on this matter always are subjective books only and never objective statements of facts. We must also take into consideration that the individual—whether he wishes it or not—places himself into the service of social forces. The development of mankind continually requires new and greater sacrifices. People's demands grow and their ability to take part in the pleasures of living becomes smaller and smaller.

We see that physicians, too, show ascetic tendencies and that they are depriving people of the right to dispose of their libido independently. In this respect, physicians act exactly as parents do towards their children. I see in this attitude the parents' revenge for the fact that they have been deprived of the pleasures of masturbation. The strange amnesia of parents with regard to their own youth manifests itself in the most absurd manner, especially where sexuality is concerned. They tend to postpone their children's sexual activity as long as possible. Mothers, looking at their infants, shudder at the idea that as adults their babies will love "strangers" and that they will be exposed to the dangers of sexuality. One mother whom I advised to give her twenty-four-year-old (wealthy) son permission to get married told me: "I am afraid he will collapse during intercourse. I can't imagine my son embracing a woman just like any other man."

I once knew an extraordinarily handsome boy. I was accustomed to the fact that everybody told his mother: "You'll have to watch him carefully. All the girls will be after him." The mother's task of sexual protection was always emphasized.

While parents are not expected to be the guardians of their children's sexuality, they have the duty to protect their children from being seduced by irresponsible tutors, nursemaids and servants. They must see to it that proper enlightenment is given at the right moment. Parents want to decide when the child should seek pleasure and when he should not, just as it had been in his early childhood. Later, the state assumes the same right. All laws serve to curb the uninhibited attainment of sexual pleasure.

This is the reason why the fight against masturbation is being carried on with such bitterness. Masturbation frees man from the social obligations of gratitude. The onanist owes gratitude for his pleasure only to himself. Thus it happens that masturbation so easily becomes a symptom of defiance against the parents. Children whose parents do not bother about their masturbation stop it by themselves. I found that *the drive to masturbate becomes most deeply fixated when the child feels that in this way he acts against his parents' wishes and then continues to masturbate out of parapathic defiance.* The purer parents wish to keep their child, the stronger becomes his animal-like tendency.

The development of mankind is based on the following formula: *People always learn to love more and to give more.* When we look back upon past times, we visualize primal man as half-beast, thinking only of himself, hating everything that presented an obstacle to his desires. Millions of years had to pass before man learned how to love. The training for and the overt sign of this love was the "sacrifice." Ancient gods were feared. Awe is a rudiment of the former boundless, primitive fear of the deity. Primal man parted only unwillingly with the gifts which the altar consumed. Not yet did he know the greatest of sacrifices, the sacrifice out of the joy of giving.

It is obvious that the need for masturbation will increase as our cultural ethical demands grow and as our love-life becomes more refined. The need for masturbation increases as it becomes more difficult to discharge libido within the environment. We can imagine an era in which masturbation played only a minor role. Primal man knew no barriers and seized every erotic pleasure he could find. With the development of the ethical imperative, "You must not!" libido had to be sought in an auto-erotic way.

I consider myself part of the great social movement which now urges greater sexual freedom. But I am not deluding myself and I do not believe that this is the beginning of an era of free and uninhibited sex life. The development of mankind goes into a different direction and continually demands new sacrifices of instincts. We physicians see the victims of these terrible struggles and must attempt to attend those that have been wounded. We are only Samaritans. No matter how many individuals our activities may save—the fight is not going to stop.

Substitutes are found for the pleasure that was lost in the surrender of auto-erotic instincts. Sexual energies sublimate themselves. Man finds new sources of pleasure in the enjoyment of beauty, of nature, of art, in the joy of giving, in social activities.

Mysterious, unknown forces are at work within ourselves and lead us toward distant goals that we can only dimly fathom. How tangled are the strings that connect past and future and tie us up with the fate of the world.

How helpless do we drift in the stream of life, *carried* when we believe that we are the carriers, *led* when we believe that we are the leaders, *thrown onto* the shore when we boast of having found the safe land.

Following the success of the *Anxiety States*, my publisher was anxious to have this new book published, but he doubted if it would be a good seller during the war. At first he hoped, as did everyone else, that the war would be over within a few weeks. The time went by, the weeks, months, and years; finally he plucked up courage, and my manuscript was sent to the printer. Then the publisher became troubled about the size of the volume. He asked me to publish two parts, "Masturbation" and "Homosexuality," as a separate volume. They were already in type, and by adding some more material to the beginning and to the end I assembled the single volume. The book appeared during the war as the second volume of my series of ten volumes on *Disorders of the Instincts and Emotions*. The first edition of *Anxiety States* was now called "Volume I" of the series. I am grateful to the publisher for having stopped the printing of the whole work at this juncture. Thus I had time to enlarge the different parts, to collect new observations and to deepen my conclusions. I also obtained enough material for the next (third) volume, *Frigidity in Women*.[1]

One day I gave a popular lecture on this subject. The auditorium was filled to capacity. As a consequence I obtained rich material for further study—many frigid women, some of whom could pay for treatment and

---

[1] The English translation by J. S. van Teslaar appeared in 1926, Liveright Publishing Corp., New York.—*The Editor*.

some of whom were poor. Freud did not reckon with my ability to maintain an extensive practice without his help. However, through my articles in newspapers, my lectures, and, finally, through my books, I attracted a large number of patients—except during the first weeks of the war—and it was not necessary to fall back on my savings. I never permitted myself to be coerced by anyone. Freedom of action has always been my guiding star. After I broke with Freud, my journalistic work was of timely help. Freudians later used this fact to stigmatize me and to deny my scientific qualifications—they called me "a mere journalist." Their deprecating reviews did not trouble me, nor was I disturbed by their often venomous animosity. The new book, *Onanie und Homosexualität,* became a definite success despite the war. In a short time I had to publish a second edition. Meanwhile, *Nervous Anxiety* went into a third edition which was published without Freud's preface.

I enjoyed my work at the hospital. One day I was summoned by the superintendent to his office. He asked me if I would like to become the head of a large neurological station. The thought flashed through my mind: "Am I fit for this work?" I accepted but asked for a week's release from duty. This free week I employed, day and night, to prepare myself for my new position. I feel no constraint in confessing that at that time I had forgotten much of my earlier knowledge of anatomy, a part of medicine which is so important in the treatment of war injuries, and even in neurology. I bought two textbooks and read up on the topics in question with the zeal and concentration of a freshman. My experience at Krafft-Ebing's clinic was valuable. It was just a matter of refreshing my former knowledge. I also bought various instructive diagrams, and when my assignment arrived, I was sufficiently prepared to handle it.

THE DINNER SPEECH

Before leaving the hospital, I attended a dinner in honor of our chief. About twenty physicians from the hospital, together with the guests of honor were gathered at the restaurant, and among them was a famous man. The dinner was scheduled for eight o'clock. It was eight-thirty when someone timidly inquired if the chief had been informed about this dinner. To the dismay of all present we learned that he had not been invited. Two men went to his home, but he was not there, and no one knew where he could be found. They returned "empty-handed." We decided to go ahead with the dinner and thus save an extremely embarrassing situation. On this occasion I delivered a long speech, perhaps the best I have ever delivered. "Through this mishap," I said, "we are inaugurating a new type of testimonial dinner. These dinners should be arranged without the presence of the guest of honor. It is a splendid opportunity! Heretofore we have always been obliged to praise and flatter the honored guest; under the new system we are free to criticize him and to expose his weak spots." I continued in this vein, and finally I asked all present to drink to the health of our beloved chief, absent though he be in body and spirit. A roar of laughter followed, and the enjoyable evening lasted until

well after midnight. Our chief stated later that it was
the best testimonial speech he had ever *heard of.*

Years ago I had a similar opportunity to turn general
embarrassment into unrestrained merriment. It was
during a trip to Norway in an atmosphere of strict
formality on an Austrian luxury steamer. On the
eighteenth of August, the birthday of our Emperor, the
captain arranged a solemn banquet at which he had to
propose a toast. The captain was a fervid Italian na-
tionalist, anything but an Austrian patriot. Nevertheless, he was determined to go through with the ceremony and he began: "Though we are here in the far
north—though we are here in the north—the far
north—" He broke down and could not proceed. Pick-
ing up his prepared speech, the transcript of which lay
on the table, he tried in vain to continue. His id was in
revolt against the undesired obligation, so he cursed
and fumed and wound up by saying, "Three cheers for
Emperor Franz Josef." Some anemic cheers followed
and then a distressing silence. Everybody was in a bad
humor; the captain was embarrassed. I arose and made
an impromptu speech.

"Dear Captain, Ladies and Gentlemen: What is the
duty of the captain? To navigate his ship. We do not
care a hang that our good captain here has been stuck
in his speech as long as his ship does not get stuck. Let's
drink to the health of our efficient captain."

The atmosphere cleared—everyone relaxed. The captain embraced and kissed me, and regaled all of us with
champagne.

Ironically enough, that same night our ship did run

aground, and were it not for the fact that we hit upon a sandbank, we would have lost our lives.

A GREAT PASSION

At this time I went through one of the deep passions of my life. Among my patients I was especially interested in a German lady, an aristocrat, emaciated like a skeleton because any dish she ate gave rise to severe pains in her stomach. One of her main troubles was that after a few minutes of reading, the letters swam before her eyes. The deeper motive of her disease was very interesting, but discretion forbids me to go into these details. This lady was nearly forty, and the mother of four children. Her treatment made only slow progress. The season in Ischl—where I was treating her—was finished and I had to go home. Her companion told me, at my last visit: "You have had bad luck with my mistress. She confided to me that she feels very happy that she doesn't have to go on with this unbearable method."

I felt more hurt than in other disappointing cases, but there was nothing I could do about it. I returned to Vienna; two or three weeks passed and I received no word from her. Then she arrived. She was a different being. She resumed treatment and developed a strong transference. I yielded to such an exaggerated countertransference that I lost my poise.

The patient improved every day, put on weight, could read without difficulty, but I, her physician, was in the throes of a veritable love fever. I had never been so unreasonable. I was carried away like an adolescent.

She was fair-haired, tall, slim; the very opposite of my
mother who was dark, short, and plump. (Our choice
of love partners is determined by our infantile ideals.
Was Freud right when he suggested that I had a mother
fixation? We choose our ideal either by identification
or by differentiation from our infantile fixation. *Les
extremes se touchent*.) I was always longing for a fair-
haired girl, but the girls for whom I fell were usually
dark-haired. Now this fair-haired lady appeared to be
the realization of my ideal. Her voice was so sweet that
it was a keen pleasure for me to listen to her.

We were both unhappily married, and we were firm
in our determination to get divorced from our partners
and to marry each other. My poetic faculty came to life
once more. Every day I brought her a new poem. (Some
of these poems were later published in my book, *The
Wise and the Fool*). The following two poems are samples from that collection.

AT THE CONCERT

Our thoughts are moving round and round
Mated in floods of homophones;
What warms your heart, what stirs my blood,
Swings softly in the overtones.
You are so near—and yet so far,
The hall appears filled up with you
And all the blessings of our love
In music find their sound and cue.
Do not the chords express our longing?
The joys that cannot be surpassed?
And does not music force our tears
For all the raptures we have missed?

TO NATURE

All I have I owe your bounty:
New-born ardors, new incentives!
If I wished to float to Heaven,
You would gently bear me upward.

See, the fires of joy are blinking,
See, the cups are full and winking,
Let us sip the thrills delightful
And submerge in tender rapture!

Our hands in lavish fashion
Must expend our offerings freely—
Lust must never turn to anguish,
What commenced, shall end no more.[1]

---

[1] Translated from the original by E. A. Gutheil.

IM KONZERT

In gleicher Töne Flut vermählt
Ziehn die Gedanken ihre Kreise;
Was Dich erfüllt, was mich bewegt,
In Obertönen schwingt es leise.

So nahe bist Du - - - so entlegen,
Der Saal is ganz von Dir erfüllt
Und unsrer Liebe reicher Segen
Scheint durch der Töne Macht enthüllt.

Erzählt nicht jeder Ton vom Sehnen?
Von Freuden, die wir kaum erträumt?
Und zittern nicht die heissen Tränen
Weil wir noch mehr vom Glück versäumt?

AN DIE NATUR

Alles hast du mir gegeben:
Neue Gluten, neues Leben!
Will ich in den Himmel schweben,
Lass ich mich von dir erheben.

Sieh, die Freudenfeuer blinken,
Sieh den vollen Becher winken,
Lasst uns Wonneschauer trinken
Und in Liebeslust versinken!

Ja! Mit überreichen Händen
Mässen wir die Gaben spenden—
Nie soll Lust in Schmerz sich wenden,
Was begonnen, soll nicht enden.

Neither my inamorata nor I concealed our intention to marry, and we wrote about these important decisions, I to my wife, she to her husband. Disagreeable letters were exchanged with our legal mates, but we remained resolute. Love was stronger than reason.

The war broke out and she had to go home. At first we exchanged daily letters, then the correspondence ceased. One day, I received a letter from a friend of hers with the following story. My sweetheart's husband, an officer of high rank, was wounded during the first weeks of the war; his life hung in the balance. She had the idea that if she could give him unexpected joy he would recover. She promised him that she would give up our relationship and that she would stay with him forever. He recovered and she kept her word.

At the height of our passion our love was so strong that we had the intention of dying together if we could not marry. Later I realized that I would have been unhappy with her; our backgrounds were different and discords would have emerged shortly after our marriage. When I read the letter from her friend, I realized my loved one could not have acted differently. I accepted the inevitable and tried to forget her. I devoted all my time to the wounded and sick soldiers.

Every fourth day I was on duty for twenty-four hours. I could not forget. I was still like a man enchanted, walking about in a dream. I read her letters over and over again. Life seemed empty and worthless. In my free time I walked for hours and hours recalling alluring pictures of my beloved and me together, and looking into a dark future. I had no patience for analysis—and I had no analysands anyway.

My salary as a hospital physician was too small to cover my expenses. I employed my journalistic talent again, and the items I wrote at this time for newspapers were later collected and published as a book under the title *Psyche and War*. I was tortured by desperation, yearning, self-reproaches, and a feeling of futility. After the last emotional upheaval, the lull that ensued was unbearable. An aphorism of La Rochefoucauld goes like this: "You are never so ready to enter a new love as when you have finished an old one." The author is right. Like a madman, I was looking for a substitute. Each slim, blonde girl or woman who showed a real or fancied resemblance to my inamorata attracted me for a moment, but disappointment followed soon and I would turn away from her.

The atmosphere of war was favorable for cheap conquests. In the hospital there were many girls and women from good families working as nurses. The milieu impressed them so intensely that their sympathy with the sick, and their enthusiasm for the world events ultimately turned into simple sexuality. Many of these girls gave themselves to the servicemen or to the physicians without particular scruples and without pretending to be in love. Some them were daughters of physicians or men in high positions, even of aristocrats; the fact that they were permanently working with men, and that war brought the theme of death into the foreground of their consciousness must have produced this effect.

Alas, the war lasted for years; my son, a young and gifted musician, had to join the army and after a short training period was sent to the front lines.

The last year of the war was horrible. I had no cause

to complain about lack of food. I was able to obtain enough meat and bread at the hospital. There were smugglers, black marketeers who could furnish almost everything, but at fantastic prices. The cost of living increased enormously from day to day and the population suffered greatly. More bread was needed; my wife went to one of those private bargainers, and in exchange for a part of the layette of one of our children, received some provisions. It was an incongruous sight later to see the child of these otherwise poor people clad in laces and silks. The conditions affected also the morals of the individual. If anyone made a new acquaintance he was involuntarily haunted by the thought, "What can I get from this man? What can I use him for?"

I had a patient who boasted of his erotic experiences during the war. He used his great store of sugar and flour to make easy conquests among women. He would accost a woman on the Ringstrasse, saying, "You look very pale! What do you need? Sugar? Flour? Meat? I can provide you with everything you need." So for two pounds of sugar he obtained what he wanted.

I liked my work at the hospital. The gossip of my personal opponents among the Freudians was perhaps the reason why my colleagues at the hospital at first doubted my scientific qualifications, but in a short time they changed their minds, and we became good friends. On duty days, when not disturbed by visitors, I used my free time for correcting proofs, for writing and for studying. Oh these visitors! They became a terrible nuisance. All my "flames," all my acquaintances (and I had so many) found out that I was on duty every fourth day. They seized the chance for a visit to my private room. They disturbed me in my work, and while I was yearning for true love, I was not always able to free myself from passing flirtations.

At last I met a charming young woman. She later became my fate and my fulfillment—Hilda, my present wife. I decided to break off all liaisons except the one with this woman who appealed to me mentally. (Mother of two children, she was unhappily married and was about to get a divorce.)

I had only one thought, to marry my loved one as quickly as possible. She became my best collaborator. She corrected my proof-sheets, gave me many ideas for my new book, *Frigidity in Women,* and developed a great analytic ability. I used her as an assistant in psychoanalysis. Was her healing ability inherent in her, or did she learn by constant contact with me? At any rate, her skill and intuition were outstanding.

A short time later I had a second assistant, Emil A. Gutheil. He was then a student of medicine. He wrote a letter to me asking for my opinion about one of his dream interpretations. I noticed that he had great talent for psychotherapy, invited him to call on me, and gradually he became my collaborator. He had very limited means and although he was still a student, I referred enough cases to him so that he was able to earn his living. He became one of my best pupils. (He is now practicing psychoanalysis in New York.) I was much impressed by the integrity of his character and observed that he never flattered me, that he never behaved like some of the sycophants I had to deal with. He was efficient in his work and always loyal and faithful.

Without the help of my present wife I could not have

come through the horrors of the war and post-war period. She had a warm and sympathetic understanding of mankind and shared my ideas of humanity. I gave her the pet name of "Gulf" from the warm Gulf Stream that flows through the ocean from the Gulf of Mexico to Iceland. Every Sunday we went for a hike through the hills around Vienna. We were both very happy; we liked to discuss and exchange ideas. At first, I appreciated her naïveté and simple kindness, and soon I was delightfully surprised to find that she was a person of high intellectual attainments, and that her interests and ideals corresponded with my own.

WAR'S END

The last winter of the war was the most severe I ever experienced. The food was poor in quality; there were so many substitutes that we all were more or less undernourished. My room at the hospital was barely warm, and the wards were cold. We did not have enough fuel and the large rooms with their wooden walls and large windows would not get comfortably warm even with constant heating. The temperature in the wards was a few degrees below freezing; the patients had to lie in bed fully clothed, and covered by blankets, but they were happy not to be in the trenches. There followed horrible weeks in which an epidemic disease called Spanish influenza mowed down the strongest like grass before the scythe. The doctors, too, were infected, and we, the heads of the departments, at other times free from night duties, remained alternately overnight in the hospital.

One night, when I was on duty, twenty soldiers from Bosnia, most of them strong, athletic men, died, whereas many weaklings made a successful fight for life.

A short time prior to the end of the war I was ordered to go to Bosnia.[1] There was a shortage of physicians there and I was to be assigned to duty at an isolation hospital at Sarajevo. I was desperate. To leave my familiar hospital, the hospital I needed for the writing of my new book, and to go so far away from the woman I loved! I went to the physician in charge of the medical service in the Army; he was very kind. He knew it was absurd to send me to Bosnia since he had no substitute for my services in Vienna, and it was stupid to transfer me to an isolation hospital where the work was new to me.

"What kind of cases are taken there?" I asked.

"It's a hospital for spotted fever."

"But I have hardly any experience with such epidemics. I am not afraid of infection, but I am a *psychiatrist*."

"It doesn't matter. You are a soldier and have to go where you are sent. However, if you can get me a substitute, a doctor who is willing to go to Bosnia, you can remain here."

We were receiving twenty *kronen* a day at our hospital while a doctor at an isolation hospital would receive thirty *kronen*. But what did money mean to me at this point! I had just published my third volume of the *Disorders of the Instincts and Emotions, Frigidity in Women,* and the fourth volume, *Impotence of the Male,*

---

[1] Now a province of Yugoslavia.—*The Editor.*

DR. EMIL A. GUTHEIL

was almost ready. I had to get out of the assignment. Worried, I left the office. Just outside the gate a colleague addressed me, a man who had heard one of my lectures. He was a war refugee who now lived in Vienna with his wife and two children. He was completely destitute and was eagerly seeking a job. "I can offer you one," I said joyfully. "How would you like to earn thirty *kronen* and board a day!"

"It can't be possible!" he cried, "You are my savior!" He became my substitute. Shortly afterwards, the war came to an end.

BACK TO CIVILIAN LIFE

Armistice Day—what joy! In the same mood, I have greeted the first blossoming tree after a severe winter. The sufferings of the population were beyond endurance. The bones of many of the people had become soft from dietary deficiencies; the streets were filled with cripples.

The first weeks after the armistice were electrifying. Revolution was in full swing; there was street fighting, and it was dangerous to be out after dark. These risks did not deter me from going to see my dear Gulf every night. We discussed our divorce difficulties. My wife asked such an enormous alimony that I could not see any way out. Through devaluation I had lost all my savings during the war. The war bonds were worthless. The problem was how to obtain the capital for the divorce, and for the establishment of a new home.

At this juncture, one of my English patients, Harold Coxeter, now dead, made me an offer so kind that I shall never cease to be grateful. Having heard that my divorce was blocked by my wife's demands for alimony, and having a strong admiration for the lady who was to become my second wife, Coxeter offered to advance the necessary sum if I could pledge myself to pay the interest on a loan he would effect at the bank.

I was strongly tempted to accept this generous proposal, but Gulf would not hear of my assuming such an obligation. She persuaded me to refuse with heartfelt thanks. (Following Coxeter's untimely death, his widow and her mother, Mrs. Gabler, have been two of my best friends.)

At this point let me consider the question of responsibility for the unhappiness of my first marriage. Far be it from me to repudiate my share of responsibility. I have, indeed, stressed the merits of my first wife. She was a woman of fine qualities, and it was natural that I was attracted to her. But the best man and the best woman in the world may fail to amalgamate properly in married life. ("You marry a woman you love," a famous English novelist remarked, "to find next morning that you have married a stranger.") In our case, my wife and I, after our marriage, developed in different directions, whereas Hilda and I have drawn closer together, finding more and more in common, working in the same field, having and developing common interests, and a common outlook upon the world. In my book, *Marriage at the Crossroads*, I expound the prerequisites for a happy marriage. Here I should like to emphasize once more that mine was indubitably a difficult temperament to get along with, that my vital rhythm was much too different from that of my wife's, and that it was my *élan vital* that often led to our misunderstandings and clashes.

Chapter Seven

A TRIP TO AMERICA

★

GRADUALLY A CIRCLE of pupils formed in Vienna and many adherents and friends came from abroad. Among them was Tannenbaum, an American who came to visit me after the war.[1] During the war, he had sent me many parcels of food. He came to Vienna to see me. He believed that he would fulfill a great mission if he could reconcile Freud, Adler and Stekel. But he was not successful in this matter although I was willing enough to accept reconciliation. He invited Adler and myself to a box at the Opera. We accepted—but there matters remained.

Tanenbaum frequently advised me to study English. In the United States, he said, I could establish a new future. But he returned home before I had time to learn English.

Some months later I received a cable from my friend Tannenbaum asking me to come to America. The cable ended with the words: "I am sending money."

[1] Samuel Tannenbaum, M.D., of New York, Died in 1948.—*The Editor*.

I had never accepted invitations to go abroad. I was always too busy, and my work on *Disorders of the Instincts and Emotions* was too important to me. I was different from Adler, who went all over the world and was the most successful propagandist for his theories. But now I had to accept this offer. I needed money for my divorce. I had only a short time left in which to study English. In her youth, Gulf had studied this language for a short time, but she did not know enough to become my teacher.

So we went to a well-known English teacher. This woman thought I should learn grammar from the beginning. I have never picked up a language by studying its grammar. I learned foreign languages by reading and by conversation. I asked her to converse with me. "You will never speak English," she said with irritation. But I decided to pursue my customary plan. I began by translating Shakespeare's *Julius Caesar* and I spoke English as best I could with my future wife. She corrected my pronunciation with inexhaustible patience. The pronunciation of English, how difficult! To a foreigner, English spelling is a "teaser"; one has to memorize the spelling of every new word. Nevertheless, I made a little progress; I was able to use a few words. Again chance helped me unexpectedly: I got a new teacher, an American physician. He wanted to study psychotherapy. His means were modest, and I proposed that we should exchange services. "I'll give you the psychiatric lectures in English, and you will correct my mistakes." I realize now that he had the worst accent I ever came across, but for me it was the purest English—I knew no better. I gave him my lectures which he seldom corrected; in-

stead, he repeated again and again, "You are doing very
well." He was married, and one day he showed me a
letter from his wife, in which she mentioned having
made the acquaintance of a very nice neighbor. At the
end of the letter was the sentence, "He is as lonely as I
am." The "n" of the "lonely" was written over a
scratched "v." I gave him a discourse on "slips of the
pen" and explained how Freud had found out that
there was always an underlying motive for such errors.
He became very upset and shouted, "I'll find out all
about it. If this is true with her I'll get rid of her and
that rich fellow will have to pay me twenty thousand
dollars." He hired a detective and procured evidence of
his wife's infidelity. Then he returned home, secured
a divorce, and collected twenty thousand dollars dam-
ages for the alienation of his wife's affections. Later I
regretted having used his letter as an illustration for a
lecture on "freudian errors."

Soon I received a thousand dollar check from Tannenbaum. I booked passage on an English boat and a
few days later I was on my way.

I arrived in Antwerp, my port of departure, two days
before the boat sailed. It was shortly after the war, and
I was one of the first Austrians permitted to travel to
America. The first hospital in which I served during
the war was a Red Cross hospital, and I was twice deco-
rated by the Red Cross. I carried a recommendation
from the Red Cross office which enabled me to travel
as a member of this international organization. In Antwerp I found so much animosity towards Germans and
Austrians that I took care to speak only English. I spent
some enjoyable hours in Brussels as I walked in the old

National Square and visited the Royal Museum of Fine Arts.

My ship touched at Southampton. Waiting there to see me was my good friend and former pupil, Rosalie Gabler, who had made the English translation of my book, *Anxiety States*. When the war ended she had sent me many parcels of food, and now she feared I might not have enough food on the boat. There she was with a basket of chocolates, apples, and other delicacies. During our enjoyable conversation, she seized the opportunity to ask me for a definition of the unconscious. It was a dark night and a searchlight was playing round the harbor. "Look around," I said. "You can see only what the searchlight illuminates. There are many other objects in the harbor, but you see only those on which the light falls. Our consciousness is like the harbor. We are able to see things only when our attention is directed to them. Other thoughts are not unconscious and while not perceptible, they are always able to come back into consciousness."

Rosalie Gabler is now a well-known psychotherapist; she never visits me in London without bringing some gift. Some people are "takers." She is a "giver."

For a long time I had been yearning for an ocean voyage. I reclined in a deck chair where I studied English and enjoyed the rhythmic action of the boat. There were a lot of Americans aboard, and I found it difficult to understand them. I exchanged some words with the Captain, found that I could understand his English and that he understood what I said.

The food on the English boat was very rich, but not at all to my liking. All the dishes tasted alike, and I understood, then, why English people use so many different spices and sauces which are less known on the continent.

NEW YORK

In New York my friend Tannenbaum met me at the pier, and after the necessary formalities at the customs, he brought me to his apartment. Tannenbaum was surprised that I was able, more or less fluently, to converse with him in English. I told him that I wanted to see New York at night, especially Broadway. This was not possible, however, since he had arranged for me to speak at the Women's University Club. Evening dress was required, so I had to await the arrival of my trunk. (It was the only time I wore evening clothes in America.) At last we were able to go to the club. I had expected a reception by a committee. Instead, I entered a small room where I was introduced to four elderly women who wore large spectacles. After the usual formalities, these women began a barrage of questions about starvation in Vienna, about the unconscious, about transference. By this time I was bored and tired. I understood that Tannenbaum had promised these ladies to bring a "well-known analyst" (my name was already known in America) to his acquaintances. These women grasped the opportunity to squeeze me like a lemon.

For some time I had been suffering from urinary trouble due to hypertrophy of the prostatic gland. I had to empty my bladder soon after the desire manifested itself. I noticed that in the streets of New York there was a lack of public comfort stations. A friend of

Tannenbaum advised me that in such emergencies I should go to the nearest hotel, adding, "This is a country where you have to be the master of your bladder." The next day he became my guide to the curiosities of New York. He availed himself of the opportunity to speak about the conflict he had with his father, and to ask my help. (Later in Chicago I met his father and was able to reconcile father and son.) The elderly man was at loggerheads with his boy for having married without his permission. (At the time of the marriage the disobedient son was forty years old!)

What did I want to see first? You can perhaps guess. It was the Metropolitan Museum of Art. I was astonished to find in one room over twenty Rembrandts. I enjoyed the collection of famous French painters. I was so engrossed that I forgot all about my bladder trouble; but my guide, Mr. S., wanted to use a comfort station. It was then twelve o'clock and the attendant would not permit him to use the men's room as the gallery was closed from twelve to two. While the poor man wriggled in pain, we hired a taxi and went to Central Park where such a station was available. The attendant told him that this so necessary commodity would not be opened till the first of May. Again a taxi, and with many admonitions to the driver to hurry, we arrived at the releasing place in a subway lavatory. This was my first experience of such a kind. Mr. S. had identified himself with me and always waited for me to ask for a comfort station. Through auto-suggestion and fear, he unconsciously played my part.

Tannenbaum urged me to go to Chicago as soon as possible as he wished me to see a difficult case there. He also wanted me to see some of his New York cases. At the same time I had lecture engagements. On the third day after my arrival in New York, I left on the "Century" for Chicago. I had an upper berth and was astonished that a pretty young lady was the occupant of the lower berth. Was this a mistake? But the porter told me that everything was quite normal. During the day, the young lady and I were seated together. We viewed the scenery as the train sped along. Finally, tired of gazing, I tried to read my English book and to use the dictionary. The lady also read, looked at the rushing landscape and yawned occasionally. I had been cautioned that it was not customary to address strange women in America. Nevertheless, I engaged the lady in conversation. She appeared pleased, and inquired as to my profession and destination. I told her that I was a foreigner, a psychiatrist, on the way to lecture in Chicago. She in turn told me that she was newly married and was on her way to Chicago to act as a bridesmaid at a friend's wedding. I received the impression that she was not too happy in her marriage. Then she talked about her father who suffered from a nervous condition, and asked if I would be willing to see him in New York before returning to Vienna. Then we both retired. (I found it was most uncomfortable to undress behind the curtains of the berth.)

Later I received several letters in which the lady reminded me that I had promised to see her father upon my return to New York.

This was during prohibition; liquor was taboo; soliciting by prostitutes was against the law. Everything was sham morality. In reality, life was different. It is impossible to repress instincts by laws; ways or means will always be found for their gratification. The unenforced prohibition law became a danger even for girls of good families.

CHICAGO

In Chicago I was met at the station by my patient who soon became my friend. He was a member of a highly intellectual literary group (many of whose members later became my patients).

It was a distinct relief that my friend assumed all financial arrangements. Through consultations I had earned in a few days more than I did in an entire month in Vienna. I worked from early morning until late at night. At the end of two weeks I delivered my first lecture before the Neurological Society. The hall was crowded. The doctors present had heard that the lecturer could barely speak English. They were prepared for a good laugh. But I had learned to juggle my limited vocabulary so skillfully that I came through the ordeal with flying colors. I spoke on "Impotence in the Male." Among other points I explained that for men of a certain age their secretaries and stenographers constitute an emotional danger. I said, "If a married man over forty comes into your office and complains of impotence, watch for his stenographer." A roar of laughter followed; unwittingly I had touched a vulnerable spot. I later learned that at that time a famous professor had been dismissed from a university because of an affair with his stenographer.

The lecture made me popular, and I received so many

invitations from my colleagues for lunch and dinner that I was unable to accept them all. These invitations became a nuisance. My friends urged me to accept, as it was important to make contacts. I had no time to dress formally, and so all invitations were accepted with the stipulation that there would be no formalities. But alas, as during my first evening in New York, there was always a contingent of elderly ladies, wearing horn-rimmed glasses, in urgent search of information. I therefore added a second condition to the acceptance of invitations, and that was that I was to be spared the ordeal of endless questions.

Luncheon was usually at some Viennese restaurant, to which I was taken by car, and where the entire group ate. My friends usually rolled dice to determine who was to pay the bill—I was never permitted to pay. These luncheon parties were time-consuming, and I did not have any time to spare. I preferred to eat in my hotel.

My position was a very delicate one. We had been taught by Freud that a psychoanalyst should not be in private contact with his patients. I was with my group all the time. On Sundays we made excursions. I had to be very careful not to show any preference, not to talk longer to one than to the other. Everyone wanted to draw me into a corner for some private communication. I had to bear in mind the factor of human jealousy.

Among my acquaintances there was a pretty girl. One day, while taking a walk, I noticed her leaning from her window, waving and beckoning me to wait. She came down and taking my arm, commenced to talk about her life. She was twenty-six years old and had had no affairs with men. She was not like other modern girls who have various experiences before marriage; she would give herself only to a man she could esteem. She went on to say that one of my patients, Judge D., had evinced great interest in her but had never proposed marriage. I expressed the hope that I might be able to induce Judge D. to become engaged to her. D. was a man of thirty who had courted several girls apparently with the intention of marriage. But he always backed out. He was a typical doubter and wanted to be cured as it was high time for him to found a family. He had a strong mother fixation. His mother could not go to sleep without a good-night kiss from her son. He took a room in my hotel. Sometimes we were at work together until late, sometimes the weather was bad, but nevertheless, D. had to run to his mother's hotel to give her the usual good-night kiss.

Once he brought me the following dream:

I am in a room with many lamps. There are several switches. I try to switch on a light, try one lamp after another, but they do not work. I call the electrician and he informs me that there is a tungsten bulb among the other lamps. He removes the tungsten lamp, telling me that now everything will be all right. He leaves my room with Queen Victoria, whom I had not noticed before. I then try the various switches and am glad to find that they are all in order.

I gave him the interpretation of the dream. I am the electrician, and the tungsten lamp is the symbol of his mother. His attachment to his mother prevents him from marrying. Queen Victoria is his mother, too. This is what we call a *doublet* (repetition of symbol), stressing the importance of the mother complex. He mar-

velled at this simple interpretation. Three days later
the girl came to my room, handed me a big bunch of
roses, embraced me, and kissed me. She said, "I am engaged to Judge D., and I am so happy! I know that this
is your work and I shall always be grateful for what you
have done."

I should mention that the literary group held weekly
meetings. There were discussions of prominent books
and I always had the last word. Every one present lis-
tened to my words as to the words of a prophet. I had
to be careful not to let this blind adulation go to my
head. Sex topics were discussed without restraint. I received the impression that many women were taking
advantage of psychoanalysis to lessen their usual social
restraint.

I was, of course, not the only psychoanalyst in Chicago. Analysis was popular among the upper middle-
class and the intellectuals in this city. Even laymen
and quacks turned to the new science in the hope of
earning a good income; a one-time barber lectured to
large audiences. Advertisements appeared in the newspapers: "Do you want to be successful? Do you want
to be energetic? Do you want to be rich?—Come to my
office to be analyzed."

The last lecture I delivered at the University of Chicago dealt with "Psychoanalysis, Its Limitations, and
Its Abuses."

THE FUTURE OF PSYCHOANALYSIS

In my lecture I maintained that psychoanalysis can
bring about liberation from moralistic hypocrisy, that

it can bring about educational reforms and a transformation of social life, if it actually becomes common knowledge. People would then become so imbued with it that they would behave as though they had been analyzed to the very depths of their souls.

Truths must become integral parts of the individual personality. They must penetrate the innermost soul and must be accepted and worked through until they become our own truths. Wisdom that comes from the outside often remains on the surface and produces a misleading semblance of knowledge which actually is not knowledge but its reflection.

Unfortunately, I have found that psychoanalysis has entered the minds of the masses without having been assimilated and that it has remained there like a foreign body. It has as yet been unable to change existing prejudices and attitudes, unable to eliminate inhibitions and to create a new way of seeing the world.

I consider this a grave peril to the wonderful science of psychoanalysis, and for this reason alone I wish to sound a warning. I fear the reaction that will follow in the wake of this "epidemic," a reaction that will present a great danger for the progress of psychoanalysis. Various charlatans and quacks have already obtained a hold on analysis. The American curiosity for everything new is exploited to the detriment of psychoanalysis. Newspaper advertisements recommend books for self-analysis.[2]

Analysis can never become a mass enterprise. It will

---

[2] The following advertisement is an example: *Getting What We Want* by David Orr. "Do you believe yourself the helpless victim of circumstances? Then read this book. It tells you how to psychoanalyze yourself. $2.25 everywhere. Harper & Brothers, New York."—*The Editor.*

always remain an individualistic science. At the most,
pedagogic and reformatory ideas can be spread in clinics and mental hygiene centers. Questions of education
and sex can be discussed publicly to some degree for the
benefit of parents.

Freud has compared analysis to a laparotomy. But
this operation requires a great deal of time. Yet many
people imagine that they have been through an analysis
after they have talked to an analyst for a few hours. I
have repeatedly heard people remark: "I have been
analyzed. But it did not help me." I then inquired further and learned that the so-called analysis had lasted a
few days. Analysis is a difficult educational task requir-
ing time and patience. Communication of truth to the
patient is by itself not sufficient.

Unfortunately, it is an often proven fact that not
everyone is fit to be an analyst. There are many who
strive to belong to this profession but only a few are
chosen. The basis is a thorough medical training and an
exhaustive knowledge of neurology and psychiatry. I
have met many analysts who had never seen a psychiatric
ward. How can such a physician distinguish an incipient
schizophrenia from hysteria, somatic infantilism from
psychosexual infantilism, or a compulsion parapathy
from paranoia? How can he distinguish a real gastric
disease from a parapathic one?

Even the most experienced analysts are occasionally
mistaken. A 34-year-old woman, married twelve years,
was once referred to me by a colleague for analytic
treatment of a "psychogenic depression." She had just
come from a sanitarium to which she had been sent by
a neurologist with a diagnosis of "melancholia." Since

I was too busy to accept her as a patient I referred her to a colleague who was at that time taking his psycho-analytic training with me. He reported that the patient had good chances of recovery. Her conflicts were quite obvious. Her attitude toward her husband was indifferent and rather antagonistic. On the other hand, she adored her brother and continually praised his abilities, his kindness, and good looks. However, my colleague soon informed me that the patient had expressed suicidal intentions which frightened him and that he was afraid to assume the responsibility for such a severe case.

I asked the patient to come to my office and wanted to treat her personally. I devoted the first few sessions to a careful scrutiny of her history. She told me something which she had kept a secret from her husband: her menstruation had stopped when she was eighteen. For two years she had a slight glycosuria which did not respond to any kind of diet. Whenever she was upset she had sugar in her urine which vanished, except for slight traces, in normal times. I also noticed the bluish hue of her complexion. She told me that in recent years she had developed an annoying growth of hair on her face. She pulled the hairs out daily with a fine tweezers. She also informed me that whereas she had been very passionate during the early years of her marriage, she was now unable to derive any pleasure from intercourse. She blamed her husband's deficient potency. Yet she had to admit that other attempts, such as masturbation, had also failed to bring about any libidinal reaction. Something had died within her.

Her mental symptoms consist of considerable restlessness and irritability. In the manner of all melancholics, the patient reproaches herself for having committed errors which make her worthless. She sympathizes with her husband because he has such a useless wife. She is often unable to sleep and cries easily. She has suicidal ideas. However, she does not want to cause her husband, and especially her brother, such embarrassment.

The diagnosis was not difficult to make. Diabetes, amenorrhea, change in sexual feelings, as well as the emotional disturbances all pointed to the pituitary gland. Her husband confirmed that her face had slightly changed, that her lips and her tongue may have become larger. X-rays showed an enlargement and expansion of the sella turcica. Diagnosis: pituitary tumor.

In view of the severity of the patient's condition and of the previous good results achieved by Viennese surgeons in this field, an operation was recommended.

Both these cases prove how important a sound knowledge of organic diseases and disturbances is for the psychotherapist. Moreover, the similarity between parapathic symptoms and those found in intoxications with certain alkaloids and internal glandular secretions points emphatically to the connection between soma and psyche. Future biological research will have to bridge this gap.

It has often happened that patients were sent to me with a diagnosis of hysteria and that after a short period of time I had to reject them as schizophrenics. How easily can the analyst be accused of having driven the patient insane with his treatment! This accusation is made not infrequently and, unfortunately, has some justification.

The analyst is in a position to make the differential diagnosis between parapathy (neurosis) and paralogia (psychosis) earlier than the ordinary psychiatrist since his interest is concentrated upon the patient's emotional life and since he is able to study the minutest reactions of his patient during his daily sessions.

Analysis will never become a trade. Analysis is a new science, its basis is uncertain, its truths have not yet been fully proven. There are no analytical prescriptions, there is no uniform method which can be applied to all cases. But as no other science, psychoanalysis demands individualization and understanding. It also demands yet another attribute that not everyone possesses—*intuition*. There is much that cannot be put into words and that cannot be taught—that can only be surmised. There exists an analytic instinct which is the safest guide. However, only artistic, i.e., creative persons possess this instinct.

An important requirement for the analyst is his complete objectivity. He must not concentrate on one theory only and neglect experience obtained by other masters of psychoanalysis. I recommend that all my students acquaint themselves with the various psychoanalytic theories and then select whatever may be useful. *There does not exist an analyst or a psychotherapist from whom one could not profit.* It is even possible to learn from the mistakes made by others. I further advise my pupils to regard every case as a novelty and to let themselves be surprised by the results. Every new case may radically alter our views.

How can one learn psychoanalysis? It is very difficult to learn out of books. The best way is to be analyzed by a good analyst. This, however, is not all. The student must also analyze a number of cases under the analyst's steady control. This means that he must see his patients every day and that he must discuss the results of his treatment with the teacher. Unfortunately, only few analysts have had such training.

We have compared analysis to a dangerous operation. A surgeon must have thorough clinical training. What would we think of a physician who would perform a laparotomy without surgical experience? Yet physicians as well as laymen who have read only a few analytic books have the courage to practice psychoanalysis. Can analysis be blamed for their failures? It is high time that medical schools establish faculties for psychotherapy so that such specialists may receive adequate training.

It is almost impossible to imagine the superficiality with which psychoanalysis is practiced by some. It is rarely possible to check on the analysts and they are careful enough never to publish their case histories and analyses. What they do publish are usually general observations and the suspicious sentence, "As my analyses have proven . . ." replaces the case histories. However, I frequently see patients who had previously been analyzed and I am always astonished at the arbitrariness with which their analyses had been conducted. Every analyst seems to have his preference. One will always discover the Oedipus complex and believe he has uttered a profound truth when he proves to the patient that he had been in love with his mother; other analysts will only find the castration complex, frustrated ambition, or the masculine protest, etc. Not to mention those analysts who are still "chasing traumas" and believe that the discovery of the trauma will cure parapathy.

The carrying out of real analysis is a work of art. The attitude which Freud has so stubbornly defended, namely, to analyze the patient without influencing him and to let him find his own way, is not worthy of a science which purports to be a form of psychotherapy. The physician must be his patient's teacher and guide him with gentle force out of the world of his fantasies onto the road of reality and work; again and again he must hold up to him the mirror of his inactivity, revealing to him his will to illness, and stimulating his constructive energies.

Just as it is true that not every physician can be an analyst, it is also true that not every patient can be analyzed. I believe that analysis should be reserved for severe cases, for those who have lost the ability to live and to work. For this reason I am strongly opposed to the movement which demands that everyone be analyzed.

I consider the analysis of healthy persons a misuse of psychoanalysis. Many people are far happier in their voluntary blindness and with their parapathic attitudes than they are after they have been made aware of their self-deception. The analyst must not be a fanatic with regard to truth. Truth is not always the best basis for happiness. There are certain lies which may constitute a far better and more secure foundation of happiness. There are people who perish when their eyes are opened. A man who suffers from a glaucoma also cannot bear the light and must gradually get accustomed to it. We must remember that a parapathy represents a process of healing, and that repressions are scars which cover deep emotional wounds. Only an emergency will force the knife into the hand of the analytic surgeon.

Conversely, I do not believe that laymen (patients) ought to read scientific analytic literature. This is an important demand at a time when every college student has read a volume of Freud and a variety of other analytic books. This objection applies, of course, only to scientific works, not to the popular ones of which I myself have written a few. These latter books are usually sufficiently informative to do some good without causing any damage, whereas the purely scientific works confuse the layman and provide him with a smattering of knowledge which may eventually prove dangerous to him.

There is one type of repression which may be far more dangerous than the parapathic repression. I call it *secondary or post-analytic repression.* It is a repression the patient carries out secondarily (post-analytically) with the aid of the analysis, after his hysterical unwillingness to see has been eliminated and he has been made aware of his repressions. He acts the part of the healthy individual who has overcome his complexes. Yet, at the same time, he retains his former attitude, the only difference being that he has concealed it even better from his consciousness.

I once heard a story which to me seems an excellent illustration of the nature of secondary repression. In a house there once lived two sisters who were spoiled and pampered by their parents. They were not wealthy but they enjoyed working. They were happy in their modest home. The only circumstance that annoyed them was a thick, high wall that stood in front of their windows and did not permit any sunshine to enter the apartment. They had no view on gardens or streets and only a narrow strip of sky was visible. Parents and children often spoke about buying the house next door and having the wall torn down. The parents died and the two sisters scraped and saved in order to be able to buy for themselves a view on the beautiful world. They were already forty years old when they had finally saved enough money to buy the neighboring ground with the ugly wall and to have it removed immediately. But nothing ever came of the happiness they had expected. Now there was too much light, they saw too many ugly things in the streets and they yearned for their dear old wall. Thus they saved again for ten years, then had their wall rebuilt and were happy and contented.

All our patients suffer from a constriction of their intellectual field of vision. But not all who have recovered can bear the view into distance. After their analysis many of them collect the old bricks and build a second wall. Unfortunately, only very few physicians are aware of that fact. Intellectual acceptance of the causes of the illness does not help against it. I recall the mistakes I made during the early years when I was carried away by analytic enthusiasm. A man consulted me about various symptoms, especially his irritability towards his sister with whom he quarrelled continuously. He also suffered from insomnia and sexual im-

potence, accompanied by violent erections at night.
The sister who had come with him complained about
her brother. He always quarrelled with her, but whenever she wanted to leave the house he was unhappy and
cried. He was jealous and never permitted her to see
another man. She, too, tormented her brother with unreasonable jealousy. I explained to them that they were
both suffering because of their incestuous fixation and
advised them to separate. Both realized that I was right.
There was too much evidence. The man had often
dreamed of intercourse with his sister and she admitted
that she had had similar ideas and dreams. I committed
the grave error of making my demand without analyzing the patient and without investigating other causes
of his parapathy. I was hoping that separation would
bring about a dissolution of their incestuous attitude.
Some days later I received a letter from them telling me
that they had come to the conclusion that I was on the
wrong track. Their incestuous ideas were only a consequence of the false theories expounded by Freud,
whose books they had read. The brother entered a
sanitarium and his sister went to stay with relatives.
Four weeks later they met again. Shortly afterwards
the man attempted to commit suicide after having tried
to have intercourse with his sister—allegedly while in
a state of trance. The girl, whom I analyzed successfully some time later, told me that in their childhood
he had played with her sexually and that he had tried
to seduce her when he was seventeen. The brother was
later successfully analyzed by another physician. Both
have since married and are emotionally well-balanced.

I once treated a boy who had been brought to me

by his father, a highly intelligent physician who had read books by Freud and Stekel and who claimed that he had successfully completed many analyses. He suspected that his son was in love with his sister. Analysis revealed that the patient had actually had intercourse with his sister for the past several years. Some time later the patient's father came to Vienna and wanted to discuss with me the results of his son's analysis. I refused to reveal to him the facts which the analysis had brought forth. He called his son into the room:

"The doctor can tell me everything, can't he? You know how broad-minded I am."

The boy said: "I don't want to keep anything secret from my father. Please tell him the whole truth."

Thus I reluctantly informed the father in the presence of the boy that his children were having intercourse with each other. (The girl was a year older than the boy.) The father was surprised but extraordinarily calm. He delivered an interesting lecture on his liberal views according to which there was nothing unnatural in incest; his children had been doing no wrong, especially since their relationship had lasted for five years, i.e., since childhood. He asked me what measures he ought to take and I advised him to separate brother and sister permanently.

I confessed that I was astonished at the father's calm and magnanimity. The next day the boy came to me, crying bitterly. He reported that his father had beaten him violently, that he had threatened to disinherit him, that he had called him a swine and a criminal, and that he had decided that the analysis should be discontinued. He claimed the boy did not deserve an analysis.

As I found out later, it had been the effect of jealousy that had upset the open-minded father to such a degree. He had an incestuous attitude toward his daughter and he had treated his son as a rival. Having heard about the incest of his son, his entire intellectual structure collapsed and he acted just like any other father who had never heard of or studied infantile sexuality.

I treated a girl who was suffering from various parapathic symptoms, among them severe depressions and inability to concentrate on intellectual tasks. She belonged to a group which often discussed psychoanalysis and works by Freud and others. Her introductory remarks were odd. She said: "I am really quite well. I think I would lose all my symptoms if I had sexual relations."

Her bizarre manner impressed me as a severe dissociation and I wavered between a diagnosis of schizophrenia and hysteria. Yet some of the phrases she had used seemed so strange that it occurred to me that she might have put on an act and lied to me. At the beginning of the next session I asked her: "Why did you put on an act yesterday?"

"I don't know. I only know that I play-acted and that something urged me to deceive you."

Subsequently she suddenly revealed a second personality. Her behavior became natural and she confessed that she had been secretly married. Neither her parents nor her husband's parents knew anything about it. In spite of the fact that they were man and wife there had been no intimacy between her and her husband. She claimed that they had no apartment where they could find privacy.

Yet the patient had her own room and moreover the lack of an apartment was certainly not an insurmountable obstacle if they wanted to give each other the necessary amount of sexuality. (Every married couple has the privilege of going to a hotel if they can identify themselves.) This fact made me suspicious of the genuineness of her passion.

However, she talked to me of her great and unique love for Jacques, her husband; she praised his excellent qualities. She asserted that the only reason why they did not live together was the fact that he was not yet making $25 a week. But he was already earning $20 and she had a very good position herself. This motivation, therefore, was as unfounded as the first had been and only served as the rationalization of an inner resistance against the intimacies of marriage.

She told me that her father knew about her love for Jacques and that he was not opposed to it but that he would not give his consent to her marriage unless she were analyzed by me first.

I recognized a parapathic trick and told her:

"You wanted to get ahead of me. You married because you were afraid I might say you did not love this man."

She admitted this. I realized that she had asked herself a number of analytic questions which she had answered herself, among them the question as to whether or not she was fixated on her brother and loved him. A dream she had a few days after her wedding, when she spent the night at the home of her parents, seemed to indicate this. She dreamed that *she was having sexual relations with her brother, whom she idolized.* (The brother had married a few months previously and was living with his parents.) However, in recalling the dream, she used her analytic insight for secondary repression. She told herself: "This is not incest, it is only a displacement. My brother represents his friend, Jacques. I have dreamed about intercourse with Jacques."

The case was lost to analysis. For her love for Jacques was only an *imagined* love whereas her marriage was a fact with which I had to deal. I consequently discontinued the analysis and advised the patient to inform her parents of her marriage. They were not particularly shocked. They provided the couple with a comfortable home and made the marriage official. I told the patient's mother that the prognosis for this marriage was poor. I foresaw vaginism and an early break since to me this marriage represented only the consequence of secondary repression. Unfortunately my predictions came true. The wedding night passed without any results since her vaginism prevented the penis from entering. After three weeks the situation was still unchanged. She remained a virgin. Her body was reserved for another love. She consulted a gynecologist who suggested excision of the hymen and mechanical dilation. However, the only advice I could give her was to break off the relationship and to prepare for a divorce, all the more so since the couple was already quarreling bitterly and the disappointed husband had given up all attempts at intercourse.

If this patient had not known anything about analysis it would have been possible for the analyst to gradually give her the insight that she had displaced her emotions for her brother to his friend Jacques.

We must admit the sad fact that *we cannot cure every case, even if our method is the only correct and the most effective one.* There will always be incurable patients who act as if they wanted to get well; who consult analyst after analyst and have themselves analyzed for many years only in order to be able to provide themselves with an excuse and to pretend that they have a will to recovery which is actually being held in check by a far more powerful will to illness. It is not an easy task to lure someone who is submerged in the rich world of his fantasies into the barren desert of reality.

We must also take into consideration the secret pride of the patient in the fact that he is a severe case, the most severe of all cases, and that he is so unhappy that no one, not even the best physician, can help him. It is especially difficult to convince those patients who suffer from psychosexual infantilism of the necessity to give up their fixed ideas.

Death is sometimes the best physician because it frees parapaths from sexual ties which they were unable to relinquish alone or with the aid of the analyst. Therefore, we can frequently observe unexpected recoveries after the death of parents or siblings.

I feel sure that every reader of my books realizes how highly I think of the effectiveness of psychotherapy and of psychoanalysis in particular. I even give therapy to paralogic patients, especially to paranoids. But I do not delude myself into thinking that I have found a universal remedy. I am aware that there are cases which even the best analysis cannot help even though essentially they are curable. I hope my warnings will not be misunderstood. The more I respect and admire the wonderful art of psychoanalysis, the more I fear for its future. I want every physician who practices analysis to be conscious of the grave responsibility he assumes. We are all human beings and we can all make mistakes. But we must make an effort to profit from our errors.

TRUTH IN ANALYSIS

One experience recurred several times during my stay in Chicago. Several people tried to fool me by telling me deliberate lies. One girl boasted to her friends that she had fobbed me off with invented stories. I had realized all the time that her stories were inventions, but I pretended at first to believe her. It is my principle to listen to my patients, to behave as though I believe them, and to await a critical moment when I tell them they should stop lying and should stick to the truth.

Once a lawyer came to see me and asked me to examine a client of his who had been arrested as a homosexual offender and had just spent a week in jail. He had been caught with another man in a men's room. The lawyer begged me not to let the patient know that I was aware of his jail experience. He had promised the client that he would not mention it to me. The patient visited me, and I did not refer to the jail episode, as I hoped that he himself would discuss it.

Analysis is impossible if the patient insists on withholding information. He is unable to produce free associations, being inhibited by what he hides, and nothing else comes into his mind. My patient had recourse to various tricks in order to waste time. At first he spoke so softly that I could hardly hear him. Then he half-swallowed his words. I asked him to speak more distinctly, and he complied with manifest reluctance. Finally, he admitted his paraphilia. Once in a while he would be overwhelmed by an irresistible impulse and compelled to go into a comfort station and pick up a man who would join him in homosexual practices. I explained to him pointedly that it was high time for him to be cured, as otherwise he might come into conflict with the law. "Oh," he said, "It couldn't happen to me; I am very cautious." Two weeks went by and still he did not confess. I told him I would no longer treat him. He was not frank, I said, and therefore any further analysis was useless. He protested that he would take an oath that he was not keeping anything back, but I did not change my decision. One day prior to my departure from Chicago he came to my room to apologize. He was willing to confess everything, and was at a loss to understand why he had lied; he regretted his insincerity, and said that he would never forgive himself for having muffed his chance of being cured.

SUCCESS

I could not accept all patients who came to see me for consultation. Had I remained in America, I would not

have become a refugee from Austria. But my longing
for my loved one was a magnet that was stronger than
money. Besides, life in America did not appeal to me.

While in the U.S.A. I adjusted a number of unhappy
marriages. In many cases I was able to rectify the environment, to smooth the discords, and to teach men
and women how to behave cooperatively. Sometimes by
finding out what was wrong and advising the right
course I was able to readjust matters in one session.

Some mothers asked my advice in matters of bringing up their children. I had the opportunity to examine a nice little girl, aged three-and-a-half, who suffered
from a habit of prolonged chewing. She used to keep
the food in her mouth, masticating it for half-an-hour
or more, and then spitting it out. The whole day was
spent in attempts to force the child to swallow. The
child looked pale and emaciated. I was also told that
there was a little brother. "Does she cry when her
brother is bathed?"

"No. She is always present and likes to look on."

The atmosphere in the home was very bad. The
child often witnessed quarrels between her parents. I
concluded that she was jealous of her brother and hoped
that he would be drowned in the tub; hence her fear
of being drowned herself, the well-known law of retri-
bution. I advised the child's parents never to quarrel
in the girl's presence and not to permit her to be
present when her brother was given his bath. Finally,
the most important advice: "Don't pay any attention
to the child's habit of 'chewing the cud.' She wants to
distract you from her little brother. Behave as if you
did not notice what she is doing."

Next day, when the child started to "chew the cud," her mother paid no heed. The little girl was astonished. A second time she repeated the chewing without drawing any notice. Two hours later she came to her mother and asked for food, saying, "I am so hungry." She was cured. Three weeks later I met her in the park and scarcely recognized the rosy, plump little girl, full of the joy of life—an absolutely normal child.

You can understand that the story of such successes was easily spread. Some people came to ask advice in special difficulties.

While in America I had the definite impression that American husbands often disregarded the art of love. Business seems to be their main outlet and they treat their married life like a part of their business.

Warned by my colleagues, I avoided any publicity in the newspapers and declined to give interviews. Four days before my departure I yielded to a prominent journalist and granted him an interview. Referring to the money complex, I explained that I found the younger generation in rebellion against the money complex of their elders. The interest in art and science was growing among the young. I was convinced America would continue successfully the mission of the Old World. In the course of our conversation, ranging from the modern make-up of women to the law prohibiting prostitution, I casually remarked that some women were now so elaborately made up and so provocatively dressed that it had become difficult to distinguish between the "decent" and the "indecent" ones. This part of the interview became a sensation of the day. It had a disagreeable effect. The telephone rang all day, and I was besieged by reporters with requests for interviews. People whose acquaintance I had made crossing the Atlantic and who I thought had forgotten me sent me urgent invitations, all of which I had to refuse.

In my hotel I was not known as an analyst, but as a pianist. (I found that in many American homes there is a piano, but the players—as a rule— are not advanced.) There was an excellent Steinway piano in the hall of my hotel. I used my free time to improvise. Little by little I collected a devoted audience, guests from the hotel, the elevator boy, the girl who sorted the mail, and a strikingly beautiful maid who always came down to do the cleaning when I played. The most enthusiastic listener was a Negro bell-boy.

Before I left, a dinner was given in my honor. One woman eulogized me because I had adjusted several marriages. I realized that before my arrival many people believed psychoanalysis and divorce were synonymous, and that analysts, as a rule, advise their patients to get divorced. I considered it my foremost duty to improve marriage relations and to preserve marriages, especially when there were children. The children of divorced parents form a depressing chapter in our times. Then one of my friends, a patient whom I had relieved from a cat phobia, delivered a speech full of exaggerated praise. He went so far as to say that Europe had sent a god as a messenger to save people who suffer. His flattery annoyed me so I made a humorous speech in which I said, "The devil in Europe was bored with his monotonous work, and decided to go to a new country where his mission was as yet unknown. He played the role of a god so perfectly that everyone believed he really was one."

WASHINGTON, D. C.

Before leaving the United States, I was invited to Washington, D. C. by the prominent psychiatrist, William A. White, superintendent of St. Elizabeth's Hospital. I begged him to invite Tannenbaum as well, and he acceded. Tannenbaum asked me about my results in Chicago. Many of my patients were his former patients and he wanted to know details about their personal lives. I also perceived at that time that he was jealous and I foresaw that our friendship would terminate.

In Washington, I delivered a lecture to the staff of St. Elizabeth's Hospital and to other guests. Tannenbaum was chairman.

That night I hoped for an opportunity to talk with White, but Tannenbaum produced a volume of Shakespeare and began to read the sonnets. I could not understand them at the first hearing. I excused myself and went to bed, but poor Dr. White, the host, had to listen to the entire series. Next evening Dr. White gave a dinner in my honor.

MY FRIEND, THE GANGSTER

I should like to interpolate the case history of Mr. B. of Chicago. A former boxer, he had become the owner

of a jewelry store. At the time he first saw me he was
faced with the problem of making an important decision. In his shop he had a dainty little woman as an
assistant. Her former marriage was unhappy. Her husband was a gambler and a drunkard who beat her and
humiliated her on every possible occasion. Mr. B.
helped her to obtain a divorce, and being enamored of
her, he proposed. The girl told him frankly that she
was grateful for his help, that she esteemed him highly,
but that she was not in love with him. However, she
added that she was ready to marry him if it would make
him happy. He asked me what he should do. I warned
him against entering into a marriage with a woman
who did not love him.

I was back in Vienna, had already forgotten Mr. B.,
when one day I received a phone call from Berlin. It
was Mr. B. He wanted to know if I could take his wife
for treatment. A short time later the lady arrived. She
was a charming little woman. She told me the following story: B. was entangled in a disagreeable affair. He
was a member of the Chicago underworld and had been
put in prison because the police suspected him of being
implicated in the theft of some bonds. He was in prison
for three months, pending trial. The authorities could
get nothing out of him; he would not betray his accomplices, the actual thieves. He was released. One
day he was invited by his accomplices to take an automobile trip. Suspecting foul play, he jumped out of
the car before it gathered much speed. There was an
exchange of shots, but the police came and B. was
saved. Now he was hiding. During the time he was in
prison he had sent his wife to Paris. There she fell in

love with a young American. Mr. B. came to Berlin, sent for his wife, and found her a changed woman. She refused to have sexual relations with B. as she was dominated by the image of the young American. In the end she insisted she could not go on with her marriage. (Esteem is a weak substitute for love.) Mr. B. came to Vienna and asked me whether in my opinion his wife would ever love him. His hope was that he could win her by kindness and devotion. I reminded him that in Chicago I had advised him against the marriage.

"Does your study of my wife indicate that she still thinks of a divorce?"

"That may be her wish. Gratitude obliges her to stay with you."

"I don't care for her gratitude. She will get a divorce."

He kept his word, divorced her, gave her a share of his money. She left for America, where she became a chorus girl.

B. came to me for treatment every day. He suffered from a colitis, but one day he noticed blood in his stool. I sent him to a specialist who found an ulcer in his rectum. He had to undergo an operation. He entrusted me with his money and jewelry as the day of the operation neared, and he made me the executor of his will. He begged me to hold his hand while the anesthetic was being administered and to be present at the operation. The operation was fairly successful; but later B. had a second and then a third operation. His funds became exhausted. He had only to write to his confederates in Chicago and threaten to "talk" and they would have sent money to him. In spite of his background the man did have some good qualities, and I felt sorry for him. He became deeply attached to me. In summer he hired a room near my country house, and he would pass my place just to see me working in the garden and to greet me. Many times I met him near my office in the city. He was always happy to see me, to shake my hand. At his third operation, I had, as usual, to hold his hand. He was given ether. During the period of confusion after anesthesia he said that he loved me passionately, that he grudged me to any human being. When he walked outside the place where I was working or resting, he toyed with the idea of killing me to make sure that I would not be possessed by any other person. He died as the result of an accident not long after the third operation.

Even love is a danger. Every analyst is exposed to the risk of being attacked by a jealous patient. I have often thought of the words of Oscar Wilde: "And each man kills the thing he loves."

STEPPING ON OTHER PEOPLE'S TOES

Little differences of opinion sometimes have importance. Tannenbaum was an ardent lover of Shakespeare. He had an excellent Shakespearean library. On my last day in New York I mentioned that I shared the belief of many that Bacon actually wrote certain of Shakespeare's plays. He was furious, as though I had committed a crime. (As if it matters who was the genius who wrote those wonderful plays.) I had touched a tender spot and he never forgave me.

On the boat coming home, a fellow passenger saw my name on the passenger list and sent a note to me. "Are you the well-known Stekel who wrote an excellent book on dreams? I would like to get in touch with you." We became acquainted. He was the manager of one of the large banks in New York, and was on his way to Europe to attend an international conference of bankers.

We had many interesting conversations and he introduced me to his young wife. He confided to me that he had married her because she was a fanatical atheist. Atheism was the main topic of their conversations. Such fervid atheism is usually a screen for repressed religion. The truly convinced atheist does not emphasize his atheism. He does not talk about it and is careful to avoid blasphemies.

The man was interested in dreams and each morning he related several of his dreams. They were full of religious symbols. I was cautious not to reveal to him the meaning of his dreams; such off-hand analyses are always dangerous. A patient must be ripe for recognition; he must go through a period of preparation (transference). It is interesting how this man one day turned away from me. I had published a short pamphlet on telepathic dreams. During the war I had gathered many experiences as a confirmation of the existence of telepathy. I was never inclined to believe in mysticism and was skeptical as far as metapsychological matters were concerned; but facts are facts. It would be unscientific

Homeward After Office Hours

to shut our eyes to the truth, however unwelcome it may appear. What is so miraculous about telepathic dreams? We know since the discovery of the radio that electric waves can be transmitted over vast distances. Can we not suppose that the brain sends out waves and that another sensitive brain may be able to receive them? I myself have had some telepathic dreams. I consider the existence of telepathy as proved. I loaned the banker my pamphlet, but I did not anticipate the results. He wrote me a short letter saying that he could not continue a friendly relationship with a man who believed in telepathic dreams. He had lost all his former respect for me.

Again I had touched a tender spot. Telepathy, to him, was akin to a miracle, and miracles are a part of religious belief. The banker did not want to be disturbed in his supposed atheism, and belief in telepathy reminded him too much of his former religion. His atheism was a reaction formation established upon an ineradicable religious belief.

Chapter Eight

TRAVEL ON THE CONTINENT

★

FOR MANY YEARS I had been obsessed with a longing to see Paris and to visit the Louvre; but upon my arrival in Europe my only thought was "When can I see my Gulf?" After exchanging many telegrams and after three endless days of waiting I met her in Salzberg and we went together to Gastein where I made my preparations for divorce.

Meanwhile, I had published new books; before my trip to America, *Impotence in the Male,*[1] and, shortly after my return, the fifth volume of my *Disorders* entitled *Psychosexual Infantilism.* In Vienna, I bought an old cottage with a garden. This was the habitation I was to share with my beloved. At this time the dollar had gone up, the *krone* had gone down, and everybody advised me to change my dollars at the then excellent rate of exchange. I was foolish enough to follow this advice and I lost what was left of my dollars.

---

[1] English translation by Oswald H. Boltz, Liveright Publishing Corp., New York, 1927.

New pupils from Vienna and abroad joined my group. I set up an office in the heart of Vienna, and we moved into our new home. How happy I was! I had a peaceful home, a little garden in which I could work, and I progressed to the sixth and seventh volumes of my major work. My children were married, and my former wife was satisfactorily adjusted. I had my own school, was busy and had sufficient income for all my expenses. What more could I wish? As a youth I never craved for wealth. But I had two secret wishes. I longed for a garden with many roses and, in summer, I wanted to have an unlimited amount of raspberry juice. These two wishes were fulfilled. I planted lots of roses in my garden, and in summer plenty of raspberry juice was kept ready for me until this harmless pleasure was halted by my diabetes.

At this time my pupils in Vienna, in addition to Gutheil, were Anton Missriegler,[2] Ernst Bien, Ernst Rosenbaum, and Fritz Wengraf. I had so many patients from all over the world that I was able to help my pupils by referring cases to them.

How did I procure patients? Usually, they were sent to me by their physicians, but I also treated many physicians, themselves, and they later referred patients. Some patients, however, came in a curiously roundabout way.

A patient from Bulgaria, who suffered from a complicated form of fetishism, learned about me in a peculiar way. He was the head of a paper mill where old newspapers, books, and other rubbish were pulped down to make newsprint. Amongst this rubbish he saw

---

[2] Since the nazification of Austria in 1938, Missriegler, an "Aryan," has severed his connections with the Stekel circle.—*The Editor.*

AMONG HIS STUDENTS (1924)

Reading from left to right, upper row: Dr. W. Schlesinger (Yugoslavia), Dr. W. Falk (Italy), Dr. E. Karpelis (Vienna), Dr. M. Puretz (Vienna), Dr. H. Wiedtfeld (Germany), Dr. L. Sukman (Austria), Dr. E. A. Gutheil (Vienna), Dr. W. Schindler (Germany).
Lower row: Dr. E. Kaplan (Lithuania), Mrs. Stekel, Dr. W. Stekel, Mrs. H. Stoltenhoff, Dr. H. Stoltenhoff (Germany).

a large green volume—my book entitled *Fetishism*. He took it home to read, and was astonished to find the description of his own sexual aberration; up to that time he was convinced that he was the only one in the entire world suffering from this affliction. He came to Vienna, but he remained only two days.

The second case: one day three stout Hollanders, father, son, and father's brother, came to my office. The father's brother served as interpreter. The twenty-two year-old son, who suffered from epilepsy, had been treated by an herbalist—at first successfully, then without result. They had never consulted a physician. They hated doctors. Their servant, a young girl from a small Austrian village, spoke so enthusiastically about her country doctor that the family decided to consult this miraculous man. The country doctor was flabbergasted to see these three Dutchmen in his office; besides, the patient could not speak German. He did the best thing he could think of; he sent the Hollanders to me. Just at this time, a trained neurologist, Dr. Arndt, a Dutchman, was my pupil. The patient was treated by Dr. Arndt. At first the patient was very dull, and suffered perhaps twenty fits a day, so we let him work in the garden of a sanitarium and approached the psyche very carefully. He improved in a wonderful way; he even began to speak German. The analysis made more and more progress, and he was cured. The religious father believed that God had spoken through the voice of the servant, who set him on the right path. Dr. Arndt now successfully represents my school in The Hague.

I have not only gained pupils, I have lost some. Fritz Wittels whom I induced to specialize in psychotherapy and who dedicated to me his book on Freud[3] with the inscription, "Not one line of this book could have been written without your help," not only saw it fitting to leave me to become an "orthodox" Freudian, but also to attack me repeatedly in various articles.

In the "American Medical Association of Vienna" I gave a number of courses; they were very popular and well attended. In addition to this I had a daily course for my pupils. Each pupil had to report the analysis of his cases. I myself spoke about my new cases, recent observations, and discoveries. It was a rich and stimulating period. I published the eighth volume of my *Disorders* with the title, *Sadism and Masochism*.[4] Translations of my books came out one after another, and this was helpful. Though some Freudians have the habit of using my discoveries without mentioning my name, I am convinced that posterity will recognize the importance of my work.

My problem now was to finish the last two volumes of the *Disorders of the Instincts and Emotions*—to find time to write the ninth and tenth volumes, *Compulsion and Doubt*.[5]

DAVOS

I always had a strong desire to visit Switzerland in winter. I therefore accepted the invitation of a grateful patient, and became his guest for two months in Davos.

---

[3] *Sigmund Freud, der Mann, die Lehre, die Schule* (Sigmund Freud, the Man, the Theory, the School) , Tal & Co., Vienna, 1924.

[4] English translation by Louise Brink, Liveright Publishing Corp., New York, 1929.

[5] English edition, edited and translated by Emil A. Gutheil, Liveright Publishing Corp., New York, 1949.

During this time I had the opportunity to finish this long-planned book.

I arose at six in the morning, corrected and enlarged my manuscript, and after a hearty breakfast I continued to work until ten o'clock. The cold at night was terrific, yet by ten o'clock in the morning it was so warm in the sunshine that an overcoat was an unnecessary garment. At first I wanted to learn skiing, but I preferred ice skating. In my youth I had been a skillful skater. In Vienna, I never found the time for this invigorating sport, but at Davos, after a short time, I recaptured my skill. I have always tried to combine my work with some outdoor sport. Until two years ago, I always managed to find time during the winter for some skating in the morning. During the summer I played tennis, sometimes in the early morning hours. In Vienna, there was a good open air skating rink (artificial ice), so that I had the opportunity to enjoy this exercise in the fresh air six months of the year. It afforded a stimulating change from my hard mental work.

While motoring through the picturesque Tyrol, I met with an accident which is interesting enough to be recorded. It occurred in front of a cemetery, a romantic spot in the mountains. I had passed it many times with one of my sweethearts of earlier days. I had often said to her, "I should like to be buried there." Later, speaking romantically of a joint suicide, we decided that in our wills we would give instructions to be laid to rest in this cemetery. In front of this cemetery I ran into a truck; all the glass in the car was broken and the carburetor smashed, but we four travelers were uninjured. Freud would term this a parapraxis, a slip of the hand caused by the half-buried reminiscence of the id. Perhaps he would have been right.

In Davos, I finished the two volumes of *Compulsion and Doubt*. My ten volumes of *Disorders of the Instincts and Emotions*[6] were thus completed. These last two volumes were devoted to the psychology of the compulsion parapathy, a disease which had become frequent.

Compulsion and Doubt

Freud had already described the "family romance." In youth, each of us builds the fantasy that he is the offspring of a prominent person who was higher than his father. Many myths confirm this infantile fiction. I could not agree with Ernest Jones who wrote a pamphlet on Hamlet and found the origin of his doubt to be a result of an Oedipus complex. Hamlet's behavior is motivated, according to Jones, by a mother fixation. I considered Hamlet's doubt to be a doubt about his paternity. Had the liaison of Claudius and his mother started before he was born? In that case the killing of Claudius would be parricide. It was impossible for him to follow the orders of his father's ghost because internally he doubted whether this ghost *was* his father. In

---

[6] The German series comprises the following volumes: I. *Nervöse Angstzustände (Nervous Anxiety States and Their Treatment)*, II. *Onanie und Homosexualität (Auto-Erotism and Homosexuality)*, III. *Geschlechtskälte der Frau (Frigidity in Women)*, IV. *Impotenz des Mannes (Impotence in the Male)*, V. *Psychosexueller Infantilismus (Psychosexual Infantilism)*, VI. *Impulshandlungen (Impulsions)*, VII. *Fetischismus (Fetishism)*, VIII. *Sadismus und Masochismus (Sadism and Masochism)*, IX. and X. *Zwang und Zweifel (Compulsion and Doubt)*.—*The Editor*.

the play Claudius always calls Hamlet "my son" and
never "my nephew."

In one of my lectures I mooted a new problem, the
patient's choice of a parapathy. Why is it that hysteria,
in former times called a *"maladie du siècle,"* has almost
completely disappeared in Europe since the close of the
nineteenth century, while compulsion diseases have become more frequent? I explained this phenomenon by
the fact that the latter diseases had a different psychic
background. Hysteria was a consequence of repressed
sexuality. The modern era of free sex life had made this
repression relatively superfluous. Fathers and mothers
feel that their children have the right to love, and that
gratification of the sexual impulse is one of the necessities of life. In contradistinction to hysteria, I found
that in all cases of compulsion parapathy the authority
complex had been shattered by the peculiarities of the
sex life of the parents. Either the mother had her affairs
or the father was a Don Juan. The consequences could
not be so dangerous if the children were not educated
in accordance with an obsolete moral code. They turn
this code against their parents. I called this phenomenon the neurotic's double standard of morals. I have
not seen a single case of compulsion disease in which
the authority complex had not been shattered. I described in detail the psychology of this disease in my
afore-mentioned book *(Compulsion and Doubt)*. In all
the ten volumes of my main work, I replaced the word
"neurosis" with the word "parapathy," and the word
"psychosis" with "paralogia," and (following a suggestion by I. F. Krauss) "perversion" by "paraphilia."
These new names are used by my pupils and adherents

but they have not been generally accepted. I used the new nomenclature for this reason: "Nervousness" has nothing to do with "nerves." It is a psychic disease, the result of a psychic conflict. You cannot hold the postman who delivers a letter responsible for the contents of the letter. The nervous system merely executes the orders of the id, and is not itself responsible. The expression "neurosis" is inaccurate and unjustified.

THE CONGRESS ON PSYCHOTHERAPY

Meanwhile in Europe the interest in psychotherapy was growing. A German Society of Psychotherapy was founded. It tried to unite the different schools. The first congress was attended by hundreds of psychotherapists and by representatives of the official psychiatric schools. I was invited to speak about the training of the psychotherapist.

I am sorry to say that there is no training that is suitable for everyone. Either you are born a psychologist or you will never become one. I have a right to judge this because I have often had the opportunity of analyzing psychiatrists and psychologists. I am sorry to say that many of the psychotherapists themselves are the worst parapaths.

What ground is there for the usual contention that no one should become a psychoanalyst without having undergone an analysis? No doubt, a perfectly normal man or woman, a person with perfect mental balance, could become an analyst without having been analyzed. But normality, in this sense, is beyond question, rare.

During the Great War of 1914-1918 it soon became clear that, as the result of the unwonted stresses, many persons who had been regarded as perfectly normal were liable to hysterical troubles which were fashionably spoken of as "shell shock." A predisposition to what the Freudians called "neurosis" and to what I term "parapathy" slumbers in us all. I have often accepted pupils who declared themselves thoroughly normal, and said they only needed analysis as the easiest way of mastering the technique. What interested me was that among these professedly normal persons I encountered some of the worst parapaths I have ever met. Having had occasion to analyze other psychoanalysts (some of them persons of considerable note), I have been interested to find that the same remark applies to a large proportion of them. I shall never forget the case of one analyst who consulted me for the relief of agoraphobia. He could not leave his dwelling unless he had a companion with him. Yet he had treated other agoraphobiacs, and believed that he had cured them.

This brings me to the core of the problem. I have discovered what I call the "analytic scotoma," that is, the analyst is blind to all such complexes in the patient to which he himself is subject. For instance, if the analyst has a fixation upon his sister, he will be inclined to overlook this complex in his patients. We may say that if the analyst is himself "neurotic," he must certainly be analyzed. Perhaps many of Freud's and Adler's peculiarities (and, for that matter, Stekel's peculiarities likewise), are to be explained by the fact that these analysts have never been analyzed, and that auto-analysis is impossible.

Consequently, there is good ground for saying that every psychoanalyst ought to be analyzed. The analyst should be free from complexes. Were that possible, even then analysis would not be one hundred percent successful, for the analysand's complexes cannot always be overcome. We must also reckon with a phenomenon known as "secondary repression." The analysand recognizes a truth, appears to accept it, but has really repressed it into the lower levels of the ego.

In this connection I must point out that a good many "fee-snatchers" take up analysis as a profession. Many a man or woman becomes an analyst after having been analyzed for his or her own parapathy, thus discovering an interest in psychoanalysis. In a discussion wherein I alluded to this, someone remarked, "Set a thief to catch a thief." But this does not really apply to psychoanalysis. What we need are persons with a good mental balance and high moral standards. Psychoanalysis is in large measure a process of moral re-education; and such a moral re-education can only be effected by a morally firm person.

We need more healthy, well-adjusted physicians for this profession. If every psychoanalysis restored the analysand to perfect health, you could suppose that the analyzed physicians would be absolutely healthy, and therefore justified in analyzing parapaths. That is not so, however. Many analysands remain parapathic. Many parapaths are partially cured, and they cling to a part of their parapathy. The contention that every psychotherapist must be analyzed to be good is, however, unsound. Freud, Adler, Jung, and Stekel were never analyzed. Who would doubt their ability for psychotherapy?

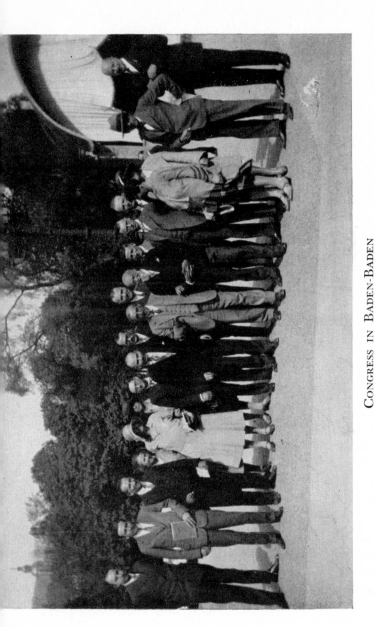

CONGRESS IN BADEN-BADEN

Reading from left to right: Dr. H. Heimsoth (Germany), Dr. S. Feldman (Hungary, now U.S.A.), Dr. C. Gerster (Germany), Unidentified woman, Unidentified woman, Unidentified woman, Dr. P. Ehmke (Danzig), Dr. W. Schindler (Germany, now Great Britain), Dr. E. Bien (Austria), Dr. W. Stekel, Dr. J. Meinertz (Germany), Dr. E. Marcinowski (Germany), Unidentified man, Unidentified man, Unidentified man, Mrs. Hilda Stekel, Unidentified woman, Dr. H. Krisch (Germany), Dr. P. Richter (Germany).

There are many good psychotherapists who use, in an eclectic way, the teachings of different schools. Every psychotherapist is an individual being, and his method must be in harmony with his personality.

The hope that the differences between the various methods could be bridged or reconciled remained unfulfilled.

At the congress every speaker emphasized the importance of his method, and the same melody was repeated like a tune on a hand organ, with slight variations. Can a conservative convince a socialist, or a Catholic a Protestant? Psychotherapy was for many members like a religion, and opinions not fitting into a specific theory were excluded. How was I to speak about the training of a psychotherapist when there were so many schools of psychotherapy, each regarding the other schools with contempt? I started my lecture. I began with the psychology of congresses. "You can observe men sitting on a bench, memorizing their lectures, impatiently awaiting their turn to speak. Like hens, they lay eggs. Then they look at the time table for the next train home." It is typical of all congresses that there is no exchange of ideas. It only appears as if one speaker were influencing the others.

CONGRESS IN BADEN-BADEN

I was invited by the famous psychiatrist, Kretschmer, to deliver at the next (second) psychotherapeutic congress the introductory lecture on compulsion diseases. The congress would be dedicated to the study of this abnormality. It was not only a great honor, it was the first official recognition of my work. Simultaneously, twelve of my pupils announced lectures on the same theme. My school came before the public for the first time as a group.

I used this occasion to make a trip through Germany by car. Although I was sixty years old, I had learned to drive, passed the licensing examination, bought a car, and gained still another joy in life.

My wife and I took turns driving to Leipzig where I spoke over the radio and gave a lecture on the *Psychology of Criminals* before a society whose members were lawyers, judges, and physicians. I saw my books in the windows of many bookshops in Germany, but in Vienna this was a rare sight. Were the Viennese booksellers influenced by my numerous opponents? I was full of new ideas, was in good form, and was applauded even by those who had been against me.

Among my opponents were many who had never read a single line in my books; they were ruled solely by prejudice. One of my pupils asked a German physician, who arose to leave the hall before my lecture started, why he did not stay to listen. The answer was, "It will only be a pornographic lecture, and such things disgust me."

"Have you read any of Stekel's books?"

"Not a page—not a line."

"You are prejudiced. Why not stay and form your own opinion."

He turned back and had the courage to get on the platform after my lecture and to apologize. He announced that he would read all my books.

I asked my audience not to accept blindly what I had offered them, but to examine the matter for themselves, since I preferred doubters to blind believers. Every sincere investigator must begin by doubting the discoveries of his predecessors, for otherwise there would be no progress in science. I finished with a quotation from a German poem which I will here replace for my English readers with a well-known passage from Tennyson's *In Memoriam:*

"There lives more faith in honest doubt, believe me, than in half the creeds."

DIABETES

At this time I was much troubled by nervousness, which was complicated by my burden of responsibility for my pupils; I had to fight against my bladder disorder, and I had an unquenchable thirst and a constant disagreeable taste in my mouth. Beer increased my bladder trouble.

After the congress we hurried home by car. In Vienna, I sent my urine to be examined; the analysis showed seven-and-a-half percent sugar. I went at once for treatment to a skillful practitioner who put me on a rigid diet. After two days I had only two percent sugar. Then I entered a sanitarium to be treated by Professor Noorden, a leading authority on diabetes. During my first visit to Noorden, the chemist came into the room and said in astonishment, "Professor, the patient's urine is free of sugar."

But Noorden ordered me to abstain from any food

for one day, and then to observe a strict diet. At this time, when the urine was free from sugar, I suffered more than when I had diabetes. I was tortured by hunger, and became so excited that I lost self-control. The nurses and doctors complained that they had never seen such a nervous man. The quick reduction in the blood-sugar had produced hypoglycaemia, and that accounted for my behavior. Since then I have dieted more moderately, have avoided dishes that contain sugar, have not eaten heavily, and as a result I have no complaint insofar as my diabetes is concerned.

Looking back on my life I could write a book on "Medicine and Fashion."

When I was a student, carbohydrates were reduced as much as possible in the regimen of diabetes, and many patients died from acidosis as a consequence of this reduction. (Once Freud told me that his teacher, Charcot, had suffered from diabetes, but he added that Charcot reached an old age because he did not keep any diet.) Later came a period in which albumin was the principal enemy of diabetics. Even later, fat had to be reduced. I understood that any reduction, whether of carbohydrates, albumin, or fat, caused a reduction of sugar; and I learned that temperate eating, combined with physical exercise, is the only remedy. I believe that my pancreas was damaged by the X-rays which had been ordered to relieve the hypertrophy of my prostate.

IN CONVERSATION WITH DR. HEIMSOTH (BERLIN)

Chapter Nine

CHIEF OF THE
ACTIVE-ANALYTIC CLINIC

★

IN BADEN-BADEN I became acquainted with the publisher Hirzel, who accepted my proposal to start a new
periodical, to be entitled *Psychoanalytic Practice*. My
pupil Dr. Ernst Bien did excellent work as editor of this
quarterly. The journal became very popular and continued until Hitler rose to power in Germany. Then I
transferred it to Vienna where it continued to thrive
under the title *Psychotherapeutic Practice*—until the
Anschluss.

In those earlier (and happier) days, a wish of long
standing was fulfilled: I was able to start my own clinic.[1]
We had four rooms where patients were treated, and my
pupils could use the rooms during the day to analyze
their cases. My pupils and I published a symposium, en-

---

[1] The official name of the clinic was "Aktivanalytisches Privatambu-
latorium."—*The Editor*.

titled *Der Seelenarzt* (The Doctor of the Soul), and our
royalties, together with the money earned from the
small fees paid at the clinic, were pooled to improve
the equipment.

Bien was a good organizer. Everything was perfect.
We had so many patients that at the beginning we were
almost swamped, but thanks to my abbreviated method,
and to the fact that we had so many co-workers, patients
were not kept waiting too long. Every student had his
appointed hours, and from early morning until late at
night, indigent parapaths received free treatment or
paid a nominal fee. Through my daily courses I was
able to supervise the work of my pupils. I obtained insight into an abundant material, and was happy to find
among my students some gifted psychotherapists.

My greatest publicity came unexpectedly after I decided to devote one evening each week to the victims of
morbid jealousy and to jealous individuals in general.
This new arrangement was announced in the newspapers of Vienna; I did not anticipate that a clinic for
jealousy would arouse such public interest. Journalists
phoned, asked for interviews, and begged to be invited
to the opening session. Many humorous journals used
this opportunity for making jokes about our clinic plan.
I saw a picture of Othello entering my clinic as a dark-
skinned man and leaving it as a fair-skinned man who
was going to embrace Desdemona instead of killing her.

On an American radio program, news of this new
clinic was broadcast without satiric comment. I received
so many letters from all parts of the world that I think
few newspapers missed so piquant an opportunity to
amuse their readers.

The day of the opening session arrived. We waited for a crowd of jealous people but only two women came. They were both *victims* of their husbands' morbid jealousy. Not one patient came to complain of his own tendency to display jealousy. Later, I understood that all morbidly jealous people think they are normal, and they consider their jealousy justified. I received about a hundred letters but these letters were mostly from victims of jealousy. The clinic died for lack of material.

BOOKS ON DREAM INTERPRETATION

For a long time I had intended to write a book on dream interpretation. Three of my books on dreams were already current; the third edition of *Die Sprache des Traumes,*[2] the pamphlet on *Telepathic Dreams,* and a booklet entitled *The Dreams of Poets* (1912). This last was my favorite; it received splendid reviews, but it was a very poor seller. In this book I made a comparison between parapaths, criminals, and poets. I found that the common factor in all three was a strong development of inherited instincts, a throwback, or atavism. Even the genius is a repressive phenomenon, dominated by the instincts of his ancestors several generations back. Every human mind entertains bipolar tendencies directed toward both destruction and construction. From these bipolar trends the parapath takes flight into his illness, the poet finds a constructive abreaction in his works, and the criminal follows his anti-social tenden-

---

[2] I. F. Bergman, Munich, 1911.

cies in acts of destruction. In many dreams of poets I was able to prove that unconsciously they were discharging criminal impulses.

My work was furthered by many translations. Almost every month new translations came out, most of them without any endeavor on my part; but now I felt it essential to get on with the writing of *Dream Interpretation*.[3] I was in a dilemma. I had many articles available for publication, but I lacked the time to write a book. So in the end I compromised. I published all the old articles and added some new chapters.

FREUD—STEKEL

This may be the time to say a few words about my relation to Freud. What are our differences?

While I owe Freud very much, as does all humanity, and while I am using a method which is basically a product of his research, our views differ on several important points. As mentioned before, one of the principles to which I adhere is that *all neuroses (parapathies) result from a mental conflict*. I formulated this view as early as 1907, at a time when Freud saw in neuroses only the consequences of undischarged libido. The conflict to which I am referring may or may not derive from the sexual sphere. It may also come from the spheres of power or ambition, or may be a conflict between the instinct of self-preservation and the death instinct. The latter conflict was frequently found in "shell-shock" victims of the World War.

---

[3] The English translation appeared in 1943, Liveright, New York.

CHIEF OF THE ACTIVE-ANALYTIC CLINIC

According to Freud, anxiety is repressed libido. Contrary to this opinion, I have formulated the definition of anxiety in the first edition of my *Anxiety States* (1908) as follows: "Anxiety is a reaction against the advance of the death instinct which has been released through the repression of the sexual instinct and the instinct of self-preservation."

In his work, *Inhibition, Symptom and Anxiety* (1926), Freud has taken over some of these ideas. While accepting the view that anxiety has nothing to do with libido directly, Freud jumped to the conclusion that every anxiety represents a castration anxiety.

I do not deny the existence of a castration complex, but I consider it an exaggeration to assume that every privation, every weaning, every loss of object, represents a castration. I also consider the habit of rhapsodizing on the theme of castration with regard to human character and the sexual development of girls as the result of scotomized thinking on the part of the psychoanalyst.

The difference between Freud and Stekel is also present in the question of perversions, which I call (with Krauss) *paraphilias*. According to Freud, neurosis is the negative of perversion, according to Stekel, paraphilia is a special form of parapathy (neurosis). I was able to prove in my books on homosexuality,[4] fetishism,[5] and psychosexual infantilism[6] that paraphilias are psychogenic diseases which are curable by psychoanalysis. To understand in this respect the difference between Freud

---

[4] *Bisexual Love* and *The Homosexual Neurosis*, Emerson Books, New York, 1922.

[5] *Sexual Aberrations*, Liveright, New York, 1930.

[6] *Psychosexueller Infantilismus*, Urban-Schwarzenberg, Vienna, 1922.

and Stekel the reader is invited to compare Freud's essay on "A Child is Being Beaten"[7] and the chapter bearing the same title in my book *Sadism and Masochism*.[8] I have also found that many paraphilias are defensive structures of the ethical ego and masked forms of asceticism. I have presented this view extensively in my book on fetishism.

Freud originally held the opinion that sexual gratification represents health and that every parapathy goes back to the repression of the sexual instinct. I have pointed out as early as 1910 the importance of the *repression of the religious (ethical) ego*. I have pointed out again and again that besides the conflict due to repressed sex, another type of pathogenic conflict is just as frequent as the other, particularly in the upper social strata. It concerns people who are able to "live out" their sexual desires and who fail in their lives because of the inner moral protest. The common clinical manifestations of this protest are frigidity, vaginism, impotence.

In the first edition of my *Frigidity* you will find the following lines: "All eternal seekers, the Wandering Jew, the Flying Dutchman, Don Juan, Faust, are searching for an unattainable ideal of themselves which they have formed in the course of their lives." And then: "Our ideal is the sum total of ego-ideal plus the beloved figures of our childhood which imparted to us our first sexual impressions—all these forces raised to the potential of divinity."

---

[7] *Arbeiten zum Sexualleben und zur Neurosenlehre,* Ges. Schr., Vol. V.

[8] Liveright Publishing Corp., New York, 1929.

In his excellent work on the superego and ego-ideal Freud emphasizes that "others" have expressed this idea before him, but that he did not feel obliged to mention names since his thoughts, expressed in other contexts, had a different meaning.

Another point of difference between Freud and Stekel is the fact that I have recognized the mechanism of *annulment* in addition to that of *repression*. In my essay on "The Relation of the Neurotic to Time" *(Zentralblatt für Psychoanalyse*, Vol. II, 1912) I first mentioned this mechanism. Fifteen years later Freud presented the same mechanism which he called *negation*.

In therapy my foremost endeavor is to cure the patient in the shortest possible time. I have pointed out in my article on "The Outcome of the Psychoanalytic Treatment" *(Zentralblatt für Psychoanalyse*, Vol. III, 1913) that we obtain our best results by setting terms for the treatment. In that article I said as follows: "Patients who have limited time, physicians who have interrupted their practice, employees having a fixed vacation period, offer the best prognosis. As a matter of principle, I never speak of a one-year treatment, and always attempt to get through in the shortest possible time. There is such a thing as overtreatment in analysis. The longer the patient is preoccupied with analysis, the easier it will take over in his psyche the function of a neurosis."

I have adhered to this principle ever since. Of course, this method requires from the analyst a great deal of initiative and intuition. I proceed from the supposition that the patient withholds from us the most important pathogenic facts. The analyst's intuition and interpretative skill must ultimately penetrate to this level.

The patient has a scotoma for his illness. It is the task of the analyst to cure the patient of this scotoma, to make him see what he has not been able to see. Here lies one of the basic differences between Freud and Stekel. Freud expects from the patient most of his enlightenment; Stekel attempts to obtain his enlightenment through independent exploration of the material, through the intuitive grasp of the patient's character, and of his pathological life constellation. Thus my method goes beyond psychoanalysis and becomes psychosynthesis and psychopedagogy. The physician is no longer a passive watcher of a drama that takes place in the patient's mind, but the patient's active educator, counselor, guide, and co-creator of an improved life plan which the patient can accept and follow.

To carry out this formidable task, the physician must avail himself of an improved technique of interpretation. This is particularly important in the interpretation of dreams. That is why I developed a special method of studying and interpreting dreams.[9] I attempt to discover in the dream the hidden complexes, the scotoma, and the secret *leitmotifs* of the patient's illness, so that I may help him adjust his relationship toward his family and toward the world.

I predict that *as time goes on, the difference between Freud and Stekel will decrease more and more.* It is my conviction that Freud's psychoanalysis may become detrimental to the patient if it extends over several years.

---

[9] *Interpretation of Dreams,* Liveright Publishing Corp., New York, 1943.

It creates an artificial regression and, with it, the soil for a probable outbreak of a latent psychosis. *I do not believe that there is any specific indication for a lengthy procedure of this type and am convinced that the time will come when even the most orthodox Freudians will realize the disproportion between effort and result.*

Freud was a great thinker and theoretician; I am a practical man. While Freud asks himself what a case offers to science, I ask myself what science can offer to the case. My success results from my lack of bias. I concede that every case may throw overboard all my previously held theories. The thrill of discovery from this unprejudiced approach has been a source of gratification to me.

THE CHALLENGE OF TIME

My sixtieth birthday was celebrated by my pupils who arranged a splendid banquet. They gave me a medallion made by an artist, and a large book filled with messages of congratulations from all parts of the world.

March 6, 1928

Dear Dr. Stekel:

I desire to associate myself with the congratulations of your friends and pupils on your sixtieth birthday. For some years past I have derived profit from your work and admired its range and extent.

With all good wishes for the future.

Sincerely yours,
Havelock Ellis[10]

---

[10] Quoted by permission of the Estate of the late Dr. Havelock Ellis. —*The Editor.*

From Theodor H. Van de Velde[11] I received a letter in which he expressed "joy and gratitude" on the occasion of my sixtieth birthday for all the "important information" he received through my work.

The letter was concluded with the wish that the 18th of March might commence a new chapter of my life which would be as "rich and fertile" as those of the past.

* * *

Dear Dr. Stekel:

I do not wish to be missing among the many friends who celebrate with you on your birthday. Almost 20 years have passed since I first came in touch with psychoanalysis through your writings. It was you who stimulated my enthusiasm for this type of scientific work and thus you too are perhaps responsible for my being a physician and neurologist today. You know how much I enjoy being both, and you will, therefore, understand that I feel deeply obligated to you for this indirect determining of my choice of profession.

Throughout the years when I had the opportunity to follow your scientific work, I have noticed with pleasure and admiration that among all psychotherapeutically active physicians of the Freud school, you have remained the only one who has never overlooked the connection between body and mind, and that because of the happy fusion of psychologist and physician you have always been able to fascinate your pupils and friends.

---

11 The well-known author of *Ideal Marriage.—The Editor.*

Your sixtieth birthday will, of course, not be a day of holding still and reviewing the past; you are marching forward too briskly and determinedly to do that.

Please accept the expression of my sincere admiration.

Yours,

Dr. Bernhard Dattner, Assistant, Neuropsychiatric Clinic, Wagner-Jauregg, Vienna[12]

* * *

Dear Dr. Stekel:

When I am offering you now my cordial felicitations on your birthday, I feel the desire to emphasize one thing: you do not know me personally, you do not share my views and yet you have helped me. Your great achievements are too well-known the world over to be reviewed by me. Please accept my gratitude for one rare quality—your tolerance for the opinion of others.

As I have always emphasized it here in Sweden, we, the followers of anagogic or, more exactly, progressive psychoanalysis, are indebted to you for many of our scientific views.

In deep admiration and gratitude,

Yours sincerely,
Emanuel af Geijerstam
Göteborg, Sweden

* * *

---

[12] At present in New York.—*The Editor.*

Dear Dr. Stekel:

Please accept the best wishes and heartiest greetings on your sixtieth birthday—from an ardent admirer.

Owen Berkely Hill, M.D.
President Indian Psychological Association
Ranchi European Mental Hospital,
India

*   *   *

Dear Dr. Stekel:

Following an inner drive, you have approached, independently, the structure of psychoanalysis and sexual science. You have devoted yourself to this discipline with glowing enthusiasm and indefatigable industry. Far from the official academic science you have worked out your own method under constant controls. Your researches are classical. You have enriched psychiatry with a new field.

Today, I am greeting you from afar, expressing my warmest wishes on your sixtieth birthday. The number of your admirers in Russia is not small. Russian physicians know well what psychoanalysis and sexual science in their development owe to the stimulation by the Viennese school of Wilhelm Stekel. Your name in Russia is as well-known as the names of the most outstanding Viennese physicians, Van Swieten, Rokitansky, Skoda, Billroth and others. May your creative capacity remain with you as a blessing to all those who partake of your method of helping in human suffering.

In admiration,

Sincerely yours,
Professor Michael Lachtin
Moscow, U.S.S.R.

*   *   *

I availed myself of the opportunity to make a retrospective speech. "Often," I said, "I have been asked,

Photo Pietzner-Fayer, Vienna

WILHELM STEKEL, M.D.

'How did you find time to write all those books?' I always had the necessary time." I related an incident in which my son Eric was involved. I had composed a new song and had asked him to correct my mistakes because I had never studied harmony and counterpoint. After a week I asked him, "Have you gone over my song?"

"Father! Please don't be angry, I couldn't find a free hour."

"You see, my son," I said, "That is the difference between you and me. I have always had this free hour."

Platen[13] said: "Who is able to make the best use of his time? He who has not wasted half of his life." I have not wasted half of my life. I strove, I worked, I enjoyed life; but, of course, I also had to renounce many things; my social pleasures were restricted. I seldom paid visits to others. If someone wanted to get in touch with me, he had to come to see me. And I had no close friends. The musicians who came to my quartets—I could not call them friends. The house was often filled with guests on Sundays. My wife as a hostess created a unique atmosphere of hospitality—but there was no intimacy between the guests and me. I sacrificed all intimate relationships to my work. I was isolated in spite of my adherents. I was nineteen years old when I wrote in my diary, "I have many friends and not one real one, many sweethearts and not one well-beloved; many virtues and no outstanding virtue. . . ." The second sentence was no longer valid; my wife made good my lack of friends; she was my well-beloved, my collaborator, and sometimes my guide.

The peculiar atmosphere of my house made an ever-

---

[13] Count von Platen, a German writer (1796-1835).—*The Editor.*

memorable impression upon all who came to visit us. It was a fairly old building which had once belonged to a man who had been Empress Maria Theresa's physician. It was furnished throughout in the appropriate style. My passion for paintings had also been helpful in its decoration. I had diligently visited the most noted picture dealers in search of suitable subjects. When I found one, I took delight in having the picture cleaned, touched up, and revarnished. This was akin to psychoanalysis; for here, likewise, I had to clean, touch up, and revarnish, so that the personality was restored. Let me mention in this connection that Freud, too, had a passion for antiques. His writing table was adorned with Etruscan and Phoenician vases. Nothing pleased him more than to be given such a relic from excavations. He was as much interested in the past of our race as in the early experiences of an individual.

A MOTHER FIXATION

Let me relate a case from my practice, one that affected me deeply. Once I was called by wire to a place two hours' train ride from Vienna by an ardent admirer who believed in the omnipotence of my method, and believed I could cure any case. (The same wrong opinion is held today by many laymen about psychoanalysis. It is false; there are incurable cases, especially if the reality of circumstances does not allow a new life. We are restricted by the borderlines of reality. An unhappily married woman will never by analysis be transformed into a happy one. Freud in one of his books wrote truthfully,

"In many cases we can only change hysterical misery into common misery.")

My admirer had called me to his sister. Her son had fallen into a fit of rage, smashed everything in his room to smithereens, and subsequently refused all food. What was the reason for his attack? He had a peculiar idea that his mother ought to guess his thoughts and fulfill his unspoken wishes. On the critical morning she had brought in his breakfast, and put it on a table in the center of the room. But he had a wish to have breakfast in bed. (I did not try to analyze this obsession.) Immediately, the boy went into his fit of rage. His uncle told me that the youngster had never been a normal child at home, but during the two years he worked for another uncle in Budapest, his behavior was irreproachable. Upon his return from Budapest, he grew worse than ever. I recognized that this boy was suffering from a parapathy although his behavior resembled that of a schizophrenic. He had a morbid fixation upon his mother, and I advised that he should be sent back to Budapest. The plan had to be rejected because the boy refused any change. What were we to do? Should we force him to go or put him under restraint? I have always disapproved of asylums in their present form. In days to come these institutions will have to make better use of psychological knowledge and devote more time to individual patients than is possible at present.

In this case the only urgent necessity was to separate mother from son. I advised the mother to go to Vienna and to stay there with her sisters; the son should not know where she was. The poor mother followed my advice. It was a tragedy to see the crying woman disappear through a back door carrying a small handbag. After a while the son asked for his mother. I told him she had gone away. He went to the table, and there I saw him standing like a statue as I walked out. For two days he did not change his position, except for evacuations, and he even refused food. Then his resistance was broken, and after a meal he went of his own free will, with his father, to the station. In Budapest, he was normal and a good worker. The war broke out, and he was to join the army in his native place. All the morbid symptoms returned little by little; eventually he had to go to the front. There he received a decoration for courage, but he was killed in action a short time later.

In this connection I must relate a second case, that of a patient I had in Chicago. I helped him greatly only by advice. Professor B. asked me to treat the son of his sister. She was a widow, and her only son, a gifted student of engineering, had suddenly lost his senses and was now in an asylum in Milwaukee. Physicians had declared his case incurable. The patient's mother, B.'s sister, came and told me the story. She had married as a very young girl. Shortly after her marriage her husband died; for many years she had dedicated her life to her only son. Being comparatively young and eager for personal happiness, she was engaged to a man she esteemed and loved.

"How did your son take this engagement?"

"Oh, he was pleased, and said to me, 'Mother, I am so happy you've made such a good choice.' "

I had my own idea about the son's illness, but I did not mention it. Next Sunday, my free day, we three, the professor, his sister and I, went to Milwaukee by car. A little after two in the afternoon we reached a fine building surrounded by a well-kept garden. It was as quiet as a church. I was very hungry and wanted to have my lunch. The head doctor of the asylum sent me a message requesting that I see the patient first. It was impossible. I was too much in need of food. After I had finished my meal, the head nurse told me that the superintendent couldn't see me because it was his habit to take a siesta, but his assistant would take me to the patient. We both went to the small, but very cheerful room of the young man. He was half asleep. I looked at the table near his bed and my first impression was confirmed—he was receiving narcotics. Now I could understand the calm of the institution. All the patients were doped by narcotic drugs. It was impossible for me to get into contact with the patient. I ordered a daily reduction of the narcotic drugs and promised to see the boy again in two weeks, but insisted that he must not be given any sedative on the day of my visit.

I came back in a fortnight, accompanied only by the mother and I went alone to my patient's room. He was sitting in a chair. He continually pulled a newspaper out of his pocket and put it back.

"What is it you're taking out of your pocket?"

"A gun."

"What are you going to do with the gun?"

"I'll kill him."

It was clear to me that the boy, ill from a nameless jealousy, had an impulse to kill his mother's fiancé. After an hour, I obtained much more evidence. The mother asked me, "How did you find him?"

"I think there is a possibility of seeing him cured. Tell him you have canceled your engagement."

"Impossible!"

"But you aren't bound by this communication. Let's try and see whether he gets better."

The mother went to her son and came out with an expression of triumph on her face. "I've told him that I've broken my engagement."

"And . . . ?"

"He accepted this communication with absolute indifference. He didn't react."

"Let's wait a little."

After two weeks the sanitarium wrote that the patient had unexpectedly improved. He could sleep without narcotics, he walked in the garden and he read books. It was a striking success.

His mother came to me and said, "What shall I do?"

"You have the choice between your happiness and the recovery of your son. It is possible that this recovery will continue if you will really give up your engagement. He suffers from morbid jealousy."

Poor mother! Torn between two loves, between duty toward her son and duty toward herself! She broke off the engagement and all relations with her betrothed. Two months later I had a letter from Professor B. His nephew had recovered and was continuing his studies.

A MANIC-DEPRESSIVE PSYCHOSIS

Such successes as this gave me courage to try my luck in desperate cases. One day I received a Spanish patient in my office. His father brought him to me from Madrid after having seen various other physicians. Jacob, the patient, was twenty-one years old and suffered from manic-depressive psychosis. During his manic periods he had a tendency to run away, and once he travelled to Rome where he was found destitute by his father. The father was a pious Jew and a Zionist. All his children had biblical names. My patient was named Jacob, the younger brother, Israel, and the daughter, Esther. They had the intention of migrating to Palestine, but the father had to go to Paris where his brother had a clothing factory. The treatment had to be conducted in French. My first idea was that he was suffering from a Jew-complex. He denied he ever wanted to be anything but a Jew; on the contrary, he pretended to be very proud of his Judaism. He spoke frankly about his fixation upon his mother; he had been bed-ridden for two years with chronic osteomyelitis, and his mother nursed him constantly, not shrinking from any detail in which she could be of help. The boy was at the age of puberty and full of erotic fantasies. He linked these fantasies with the image of his young and lovely mother, even for his auto-erotism. This he confessed frankly. The treatment began when he was midway between a phase of depression and one of excitement. He was not difficult to manage. Then came the first manic spell. He slept only a few hours, wrote crazy poems and formless novels, told me of his ambitious plans, and visited comedies and night-clubs. After this, profound depression swiftly intervened. In the depressed state he expressed an urgent desire to see his father. He had the best father imaginable, a father for whom he professed intense love; but I was astonished that he did not ask for his mother. The parents had been waiting in a mountain resort, two hours distance from Vienna. They knew he would need them. At first I refused to wire for the parents, but he threatened suicide. His parents finally came to Vienna and he spent ten days with them in a hotel. Then he became calmer. His father wanted to know whether it would be better to stay near Vienna so that, in case of emergency, he could come to the city, or whether he should go to Paris where his business needed him. I advised him to go to Paris. In the next fit of depression the patient asked me to wire for his father. He was driven by an impulse to commit suicide by throwing himself into the Danube.

I was a little uneasy, but my intuition told me that I should not give in. After midnight came a call from his landlady saying that she was very anxious as Jacob had not shown up. Now I began to doubt. Had I been right? Self-reproaches troubled my sleep, but nature was strong, and finally I slept soundly. At four o'clock the landlady phoned that Jacob had just come home and had fallen asleep on the bed fully dressed. After this crisis came a quiet interval. He related a dream in which *he had gone to Rome to be baptized by the Pope.* I put it squarely up to him. "You suffer because you are a Jew. You play with the idea of baptism, not by conviction, but because you want to contradict your father." (The son of Herzl, the founder of Zionism, became a Catholic. Sons often change their religious and political convictions in defiance of their fathers.) I expected a passionate protest, but my patient admitted that he was pursued by such ideas while in his manic state. In his attacks of depression he was overwhelmed

On His Voyage to Brazil (Companions Unknown)

with remorse and self-depreciation, called himself a criminal, and wanted to have done with life.

After this discovery we made good progress, but in many diseases you will find a mixture of psychic and organic causes. My patient had another fit of depression. It was his last. I visited him in his boarding-house. He was so weak that he couldn't get up. He showed signs of suffering; he was pale, a different being, and I was told that during the whole day he had taken no other food than a cup of tea *without* sugar. At this moment I became clairvoyant. I realized that Jacob was suffering from hypoglycaemia. I remembered that he was very fond of sweets, always had some chocolates in his pocket and ate them intermittently during analysis often offering me some new kind of candy: "You must try this." I ordered an analysis to determine the amount of sugar in his blood. My supposition was confirmed by the blood test. I forced him to drink a strong solution of sugar, and in a short time he was a different being; his cheeks had color, his pulse became calm, he felt strong again, and he left the bed a new man.

PARIS

Jacob went home cured. This success would have brought me many patients if Jacob had not forbidden his parents to tell anyone that I had treated him. Next year I was invited by Professor Claude, the leading psychiatrist in Paris, to give a lecture. I knew that Jacob was now in Paris, and was afraid that he would take advantage of my presence to relapse. I was invited to dinner by his father, who was also in Paris at the time. I met father and son in a restaurant. After some general remarks, Jacob said, "What do you think cured me?"

I knew this was a critical moment, and that much depended on my answer.

"What cured you? I believe it was your desire to be normal. You were tired of your disease. It wasn't my doing. It was your own work."

Jacob was surprised. He hadn't anticipated this answer, and I added, "If you get ill again, it will be because you want to be ill again."

On the following day Jacob invited me for a drive in his car. We had a long conversation, but his disease was not mentioned.

The next day I delivered my lecture at the Hospital of St. Anne. I had requested the amphitheatre, but the janitor conducted me to Professor Claude's auditorium. It was crowded, many professors were present, some from other cities. I spoke extemporaneously in French, and I felt that I was impressing my audience. Only Princess Marie Bonaparte (an orthodox Freudian) walked out noisily in order to demonstrate her opposition. At the end of the lecture the applause seemed endless. Colleagues asked for my private address, and Professor Claude thanked me many times, saying that he had been able to understand me, whereas he was always puzzled by the Freudians.

My reaction to Paris was peculiar. During the first days I was enraptured. The air seemed to be full of whiffs from the sea, which is a hundred miles away; people were kind, and the food was incomparably good.

Then I became restless, I could not endure the noise, some streets were dirty, and the smells oppressed me; the constant roar of traffic bothered me. I hastened to the Louvre and looked at pictures—but there were too many of them. At the end of the first week I had but one desire: to get away from the turmoil. I declined many invitations including a proposed dinner in my honor, and went straight back to Vienna.

Meanwhile my book *The Education of Parents*[14] was published in Vienna.

BRAZIL

Two years later I received a cable from Rio de Janeiro asking me to lecture at the Medical Academy. This was arranged by my friend Silva-Mello, a prominent physician who had received his medical training in Germany, and had also come to Vienna to study my method. Having a renewed desire to travel, I accepted in spite of my bladder trouble, which twice had brought me to a hospital. The formalities of the trip were endless. I had to wait in various offices; the certificate of my morality, required by the regulations, took some weeks to procure, and the money promised from Brazil was slow in coming. Finally everything was ready. I brought all my papers to the Brazilian consul, together with the flattering invitation from the Medical Academy. He studied all my documents carefully, congratulated me on the exceptionally kind invitation, and finally refused my visa because I was not in possession of the most important document. What was it, this

---

[14] "Erziehung der Eltern," Weidmann & Co., Vienna, 1934.

document? A recommendation from some prominent club. This no doubt seems incredible. The invitation from the Academy was not sufficient. The Automobile Club was more important. I went to the club, got the essential recommendation and finally the visa, too. The money arrived a day previous to my departure.

The voyage proved too calm for my taste. Sometimes I like high seas and even a gale. But every day we had beautiful sunshine and a quiet sea. Even when crossing the equator the temperature was quite bearable. There were two swimming pools on the boat, one under cover, the other on the deck. I swam every day, took sun baths, and in the evening I played the piano in a more or less quiet room called the Moorish Hall. The ship's doctor was often my only audience, and asked me to play every day. Sitting in a corner he wept constantly. It wasn't the mastery of my playing which moved him; he was unhappy in love and found music a consolation.

In Brazil, I had hard work. I was at first in a hotel recommended by friends. I was looking forward to my first coffee in Brazil. It was disgusting! Later I had "extra coffee" which tasted a little better, but it did not compare with what I used to drink in Vienna. The Brazilians don't know how to make coffee, but they are very proud of what they provide, and smile contemptuously if you praise the coffee of Vienna.

I had a very happy reception in Rio. Silva-Mello and his wife did everything for my comfort; various professors invited me to accompany them on trips in the picturesque surroundings; the Austrian consul gave a dinner in my honor and offered me the hospitality of his house, where I found a piano. The first time I

went to the embassy I saw a young man sitting at the
piano and singing one of my children's songs. He had
learned it in his youth in Vienna. Thus, even in Brazil,
I heard an echo of my early compositions. I gave six
lectures at the Academy and a daily course to physicians.
It is the habit in Rio to ask foreign visitors to speak to
the students in the various clinics. So I lectured in four
different clinics, giving each lecture in French.

At this time Hitler was already the ruler of Germany.
Brazil differs from North America in that Brazilians
never stress racial differences. The Brazilians did not
understand anti-Semitism, not even after the Germans
in Brazil organized propaganda against the Jews. The
third day after my arrival I was called to the telephone.
A harsh voice said in German, "I am the representative
of the German Medical Club in Rio. I would like to
see you at our club. Are you Aryan?" I gave no answer
and hung up.

While I was in Rio, Stefan Zweig, the famous Austrian man of letters, who is of Jewish birth, arrived,
having been officially invited by the minister of foreign
affairs. He was warmly received; translations of his
books were prominently displayed in the shop windows;
at the lecture he gave, the attendance was so large that
for a time traffic was interrupted. He lectured to the
Society for Jewish Culture, the proceeds of the lecture
being given to a fund for refugees. Two days later I
lectured in the same room for the same purpose and we
were both happy to contribute in this way a goodly
sum of money to the fund.

Many Brazilians wanted to send me patients, but I
could not take them for analysis. Time was lacking; I

could only see them in consultation. I am sorry to say that more than half of these patients were mental cases, and I was unable to find a well-trained psychotherapist who could undertake their treatment.

A great experience was a trip by aeroplane to the farm of a wealthy Brazilian. It was near the jungle, which I visited. The moonlit evenings created an unforgettable impression. I remember one night in particular. I was alone, standing on a porch. Brazilians are afraid to go out at night, lest they catch cold. It was winter in Brazil (August) and the temperature was like that of a warm summer in Europe. There I stood, for a long time, listening to the sounds of the tropical night—the trees rustled in the wind, some unknown animal howled—and I thought of my youth and my romantic fantasies about jungle life—all in all, I felt I could be contented with my life. From an ordinary general practitioner I had grown to be an acknowledged authority on psychotherapy; I had seen a great deal of this beautiful world.

I should have gladly stayed much longer in Rio. It would have been wiser had I done so. But I did not guess that Hitler would so soon annex Austria. Even while standing there admiring the lovely scene, I felt homesick, longed for my school, and my work, and the peace of my home where my wife did so much to make me happy. The trip back lasted nearly four hours; we were high over the clouds which looked like ruffled white sheets on a huge bed; and then came Rio de Janeiro with all the curiously shaped mountains along the shore—it framed a memorable farewell to Brazil.

Chapter Ten

A REFUGEE FROM THE NAZIS

★

I DO NOT KNOW WHY, but during the early days of Nazi rule in Germany, my books were not banned. Did they believe I was an "Aryan," or was it because Hitler had quoted a passage from my book on homosexuality in a pamphlet against homosexuals? I don't know. But gradually the wind changed, and my German publisher wanted to get rid of my ten volumes, *Disorders of the Instincts and Emotions.* A refugee publisher who had to come to Vienna from Germany bought the whole stock and paid a shilling a volume. (The original price was twenty to thirty shillings.) All my books were banned in Germany, but thanks to the various translations this did very little harm.

I was never a politician. My wife, full of misgivings, warned me many times, and advised that we leave Austria. Somehow, I felt unable to change my familiar surroundings; and when the *Advances in Dream Inter-*

267

pretation had been published, I wanted to bring out my long expected book, *Technique of Analytical Psychotherapy*. Besides, I had begun to feel the burden of old age. I had to face facts. I now found it necessary to go to my office in a car, instead of walking, and I had to rest a while before starting my work.

DOGS

I made up my mind to simplify life. I sold my house, gave up my office, and rented a new apartment which provided me with every comfort and convenience. There were two porches, steam heat, a consultation room and a pretty garden. In front of the house there was a big park where I could take my morning walks with my dog. I have not mentioned that a dog was an absolute necessity for me. A dog has always been my link with nature; it forces me to take long walks twice a day to give it a run. "Like master, like man," is an English saying. It is equally true, "like master, like dog." Dogs take after their masters. Stupid men have stupid dogs. Do I sound conceited if I say that my dogs have always been extremely clever? One of them, who could almost talk, was considered a miracle dog. People came to admire him and he became a well-known representative of his breed. But all my dogs were pugnacious and often entangled me in quarrels with my neighbors. A dog can establish intimate relationships and also create animosities. Tired of the constant fights of my dogs I asked for a quiet one, and was advised to take a retriever; but this dog was not only very quiet,

LOVER OF DOGS

he lacked all the qualities of a faithful creature. He had no sense of direction; finally he ran away and came home after living three days with another master who later accepted him as a gift. I was glad to be rid of him. He was the only exception to my succession of fine dogs.

HIGH SPEED LIVING

From my early youth onward my temperament continued to be restless. I believe that each of us is born with his own *élan vital* (Bergson). I must always be vigorously occupied. I cannot lie still, and the *dolce far niente* of the Italian has no appeal to me. I must be "up and doing." Though my wife was much younger than I, she found it difficult to keep pace with me. Frau Gabler nicknamed me "Quicksilver." A Brazilian once said about me: "He's like a man sitting on a hot stove." When I was learning to drive, my pupil Rosenbaum said I should drive with my head sticking out through the roof. Whatever I did was done enthusiastically. Conquests came easily, and I could never be bothered with a long siege. Throughout my life I have been unwilling to bow to circumstances. If something did not come easily, I tried to find something else that would. In youth, like my father, I was prone to storms of passion, but a storm was soon followed by calm. But my *élan vital* persisted throughout life. Not until I was well on in years did I learn to be patient. Experience had at length taught me that I would have to do without many things I had been inclined to consider indispensable.

The tempo of my work has always been adequate. I never wished to have a secretary. I sit at the typewriter and my thoughts flow so rapidly that my fingers can scarcely keep pace with them.

FLIGHT FROM NAZISM

Three weeks before Hitler marched into Austria, I lectured in the Club for Culture on "The Psychology of Dictatorship." Long before this lecture I had given my friend, John Gunther, interviews for his famous book *Inside Europe* which discusses the same theme, and which contains most unfavorable comment on Hitler and Mussolini. I knew that I was on the Nazi black list, but I did not contemplate flight to another part of Europe in spite of the suggestions of my wife. I believed that Mussolini would protect the independence of Austria; but should things become worse, I had resolved to commit suicide rather than be placed in a concentration camp.

It is not necessary to repeat the story of the stormy days prior to Hitler's invasion of Austria. I decided in this book to deal only with my own life. Friends warned me and advised me to leave Vienna. My friend, Dr. Henry F. Quackenbos, who foresaw the coming events, sent me a cable, inviting us and my wife's daughter to come and stay with him at his country house not far from New York. I hesitated. The day Hitler marched in, a friend of John Gunther, a well-known American journalist, urged me to leave Vienna by the next train. I was irresolute. At nine o'clock I decided to flee. Hastily, we packed the minimum of necessary things. (It was dangerous to travel with many suitcases.) Three hours later we were at the station with three patients from London whom I had been treating at the time. Many refugees made for Hungary or nearby Czechoslovakia. But these frontiers had been closed. Though I was not aware of the situation in these two countries, I decided to go to Switzerland. We were unmolested on the journey. The Nazis were too excited by the impending arrival of Hitler to take notice of us. The stations were bedecked with flags. The Nazis everywhere proudly strutted up and down. Some came into the compartment and asked innumerable and ridiculous questions. Had I waited one hour longer, conditions would have been different. By that time the questioning and examining became more rigid; travelers were stripped nude, and had to wait interminable hours before being permitted to proceed. But by good fortune we reached the Swiss frontier unmolested. The train was crowded, though not overcrowded, with excited refugees. In the corner of my compartment a man sat silently; others whispered into one another's ears their fear of not being permitted to enter Switzerland. I, too, was worried a little. Perhaps I would be turned back at the frontier.[1] But nothing untoward happened.

---

[1] During this trip something occurred that clearly shows Dr. Stekel's warm concern for his patients. When we escaped, three of my husband's patients left Vienna with us. Among them was a young woman who was unhappy in her marriage and who had fallen in love with a young man in Vienna. Her romance was broken off by her sudden departure. During the journey my husband asked me to comfort the disconsolate woman. His request came as a surprise to me, for the woman's sorrow seemed trivial in the face of the tragedy descending upon Europe and the fact that our own lives and futures appeared so completely doubtful. (Incidentally, Dr. Stekel later was able to improve this patient's marriage.) —*Hilda Stekel.*

The officials were very kind, the examination of my baggage was a mere formality.

After we crossed the border, the atmosphere changed. The silent traveler, talking incessantly, expressed his happiness at his escape; refugees congratulated each other, some embraced one another. We all had the same feeling—*we had escaped from hell.*

Zurich was so overcrowded that we were unable to obtain any hotel accommodations. I phoned Dr. S. Kroll, my excellent pupil who worked in Zurich, and he gave me the address of a boarding house where we secured good accommodations.

The impression produced by Zurich was chaos. It looked like a boiling kettle. The streets were seething with refugees fighting to get the latest extras, police officials were checking passers-by for their passports; one was overpowered by the atmosphere of restlessness.

I remembered that I had been invited many times by the Baroness Lambert to Gstaad where I had once spent an enjoyable month in the autumn. So we left for Gstaad; when we arrived there the kind Baroness Lambert had but an hour's free time for me; worried by the recent political changes in Europe, she was about to leave for Belgium.

Only two hotels were open in Gstaad; we took rooms at one of these hotels, and unlike Zurich, the place was very quiet. During the first week I wrote letters to all of my friends, and especially to America, where I had been invited to come for a lecture tour.

It was as though nature herself was trying to reconcile me to my situation. The sun shone constantly, and sometimes it grew so warm that we preferred shade.

On His Flight from Austria. One Last Look Toward
His Homeland from Free Switzerland

The snow melted, and you could take long walks on the winding paths.

Great preparations had been made in Vienna for my seventieth birthday, but by the twelfth of March I had left. However, the birthday was celebrated in a grand manner at the house of the Baroness Lambert. During my previous stay in Gstaad, the Lamberts and their neighbors had learned my children's songs by heart. I was invited to a formal luncheon, given little presents; there was a cake with my initials and the figure "70" in the center. A children's chorus sang my songs and gave a charming little play.

I received some letters from my friends, but only a few were forwarded by the Vienna post office.

How did I obtain a visa? I did not dare go to the German embassy for fear of being molested. Besides, I had to have a passport in which "Israel" had been added to my given name, Wilhelm. This regulation was imposed on all Jews by the Nazi officials.

Again I was helped in an unexpected manner. Walking in the street I was addressed by a man who was unknown to me. He was a Dr. Sonnenfeld. "Are you the Dr. Stekel who wrote the psychological books? I have always wanted to get in touch with you. Reading your books at a time of emotional trouble was a great help to me."

He offered hospitality for my wife and me, but we declined after thanking him. It was not hospitality that we needed. But he helped in a different way. He told Mr. Fritz Mumenthaler,[2] President of the Court of Justice at Saanen, a place near Gstaad, about my pre-

2 See Hilda Stekel's introductory note.—*The Editor.*

dicament. Mumenthaler proved to be an idealist, and he became a genuine friend of ours. He did all in his power to improve my situation. He gave me a letter of introduction to a prominent official of the Berne police, and the official furnished me with a certificate of identification which is valid for passport purposes. With the help of my English patients, I had sent more than a hundred letters to friends the world over. Before my letters reached their destinations, I received a communication from Mr. Fineman, then the brother-in-law of John Gunther, and connected with the cinema world. He invited me to come to California. Though Mr. Fineman was not well off, in fact at that time he was without a job, he wired me a hundred dollars. I decided to go to California. A wealthy American, who invited me to America as his guest, sent me a large sum of money. Then I received an invitation to make a lecture tour in America, but friends advised me not to undertake such a tour as it would prove exhausting and a danger to my health. So I decided to go to California, and thus fulfill an old wish of mine. We left Gstaad and went to Berne to complete the necessary formalities for the trip. Through the recommendation of a friend I obtained the address of a small, pleasant boarding house where we felt thoroughly at home. I went to the American consul who advised me to get an immigration visa, but he added that he did not have the power to issue one. It would be necessary to go to the chief consul at Zurich. At the American Consulate at Zurich there was such a queue of refugees that half the day passed before I could enter. I sent the consul my visiting card and the letter of introduction from the consul at Berne, and in five minutes I was ushered in to see him. But the information I received was depressing. The place where I was born was now Rumanian territory, therefore I had to be treated as a Rumanian, and might have to wait seven or eight years for my quota number. It would be necessary for me to visit America as a tourist. Through the connections of my friend, Mumenthaler, I was able to procure a certificate of identification as quickly as possible. As an exceptional case, I was given a return visa, which made my credentials as valid and valuable as a passport. Thanks to the invitation of the Tavistock Clinic in London to deliver six lectures on my active method of psychoanalysis, I received my English visa by wire before I touched English soil. I wished to avoid the possibility of being refused at the frontier, and was afraid of arriving in California in summer.

LONDON

I had never been to London and was happy to have the opportunity of going to a place that I had not been able to visit before. Many invitations to come to London had been extended to me before, but I was unable to accept them for lack of time. The only free time I had was in the summer, which was not the right season for a London visit.

I had again lost my savings, my furniture, my musical instruments, and a part of my library, but I received my recompense in London. On the second day after my arrival I gave my first lecture before a large audience, and the attendance increased with each succeeding lecture. Various physicians and other persons of note were very kind. Because many of my books had been translated into English, I was known here.

My first lecture at the Tavistock Clinic was interrupted at one point by a vigorous stamping by the audience. I wondered what was amiss, and looked inquiringly at the chairman, for in Vienna that would have announced disapproval. However, he whispered to me: "Here this is a form of applause, go ahead." This demonstration occurred several times.

From the very first I was enraptured by London. The spacious parks, the quiet streets which run so unexpectedly "just around the corner" from the noisy ones, the beautiful squares and small gardens, and a general atmosphere of kindliness and readiness to help—such as you will seldom find anywhere else in the world. An Englishman always wants to prove that he is a gentleman, and mostly he is a gentleman. If I could only stay in this wonderful place for the remainder of my life! But my plans were to go to America and England was to be only a stopping-off place.

On the third day of our stay in London, my wife developed a high temperature and suffered from severe pains. My pupil, Maberly, recommended Dr. Dunlop as a physician. Dunlop made a thorough examination and called in a specialist for consultation; both advised that she should be taken to a hospital the same night. There she remained for three weeks, and for her convalescence Dunlop invited her to stay with him. The behavior of my English colleagues and their readiness to help was wonderful. Dunlop might have been an old friend. Meanwhile, an immediate voyage to Cali-

fornia had become impossible. I was granted a permit
to stay in London for two additional months, and in
the meantime the doctors who attended my lectures at
the Tavistock Clinic presented a petition to the Home
Office to the effect that it would be of considerable advantage for English psychology if I could remain in
England permanently. As a result I was given permission to remain for the rest of my life.[3]

As an illustration of the kindness of my English colleagues I would like to mention Dr. Gleeson of Southsea. He invited me to meet him, and we went to a restaurant. There his first question was, "Are you short
of money?" I was not, but his question touched me so
deeply I should have liked to embrace him.

My experiences as a refugee are in a measure depressing. People fear you are hard-up and that you are going
to ask for financial aid. Their behavior changes after
the first reserve has worn off, and it changes still more
after they learn you do not need money. I could relate
some stories along this line, but I prefer to hurry on.

ILLNESS

Near the time of my third or fourth lecture in the
Tavistock Clinic, while my wife was semi-convalescent
and back at the hotel, I myself felt sick. One evening I
vomited, my temperature rose, and I experienced chills.
Consciousness left me, and I awoke in a hospital to
which I had been taken in an ambulance. I didn't know
what was amiss. I had no recollection whatever of what

---

[3] The frail health of Dr. Stekel may have been an important reason
for his reluctance to proceed to the U. S. A.—*Hilda Stekel.*

had happened. All the functions of my body seemed arrested. The physicians were at a loss, but I knew that I had to deliver a lecture within two days, and repeatedly I asked for my clothes. (I had none in the hospital, for I had been taken from my bed to the ambulance.)

I lost patience. I did not want to admit that I was dangerously ill. I thought only of my lecture and of my patients. Meanwhile, I was apparently hovering between life and death. Professor Jolly advised the injection of a large quantity of saline solution. When Dr. Dunlop administered the injection I was irritable, and said: "Why do you torment me? Let me go home." However, this injection worked like a miracle. All the ordinary functions were resumed, and I was taken by ambulance back to the hotel. My temperature was normal, and I was fully conscious though weak. My lecture was postponed for several days. What was the illness? It must have been an acute intoxication caused by some food.

This quick recovery is characteristic of my constitution. It was the third time I had had such an experience. I have already told the story of my diabetes. A second occurrence of the same nature took place ten years ago after a lecture in Budapest. I was overworked. Interview after interview, the urgent questions of my pupils about their cases, the lectures, and the unavoidable dinner parties sapped my strength. I came home and had a severe attack of angina pectoris, could scarcely walk without pain, could not drive my car, and had to avoid bodily exertion. Perhaps the cause was psychic, for there were disagreeable quarrels among my pupils in Budapest. (The leader of the group had forsaken me and gone over to the Freudians.) After two months I recovered, and I could climb mountains again. During the Great War, I had a hemorrhage in one eye; the oculist prophesied that the eye would remain damaged, but after three weeks I regained my normal vision. (I must remind my readers of the episode in Abbazia, too, where I was cured of my pleurisy in an almost miraculous way.) Spells of dizziness which I had first experienced while in Gstaad, Switzerland, disappeared without trace.

Dangerous disease I was able to overcome; but there were many minor ailments that troubled my new life in London. Dr. Gleeson invited me for a weekend to Southsea. You know my passion for the sea. I walked the promenade for hours and hours, until I was disturbed by a slight pain in my left foot. I came home and examined my foot. I found an erosion on a bunion that had not troubled me at all before. This trouble gradually became chronic. Each night I had such painful sensations in my bunion that my otherwise good sleep was disturbed. I could not bear a shoe. I took scissors and made an incision in a soft shoe, and then I could walk.

I learned from this example something of the inefficiency of modern medicine. We are making enormous progress in different branches, but in the minor ailments we are as helpless as we were centuries ago. Laymen scoff at physicians because they have not found a remedy for the common cold. It was my fate to learn the inefficiency of therapeutics on myself. Doctors advised different drugs, ointments, compresses; but nothing helped. Finally, after a few treatments with x-rays the bunion became better. But I still have to be careful. The wound is healed, but is always likely to reopen when the scar is pressed by the shoe. It was difficult to find in London an orthopedic shoemaker. At last I found one. The first pair was a failure, the heel was too wide and the vamp was too short. I ordered a second pair and asked the shoemaker to avoid repetition of his error. The second pair came with the vamp much smaller and the heel still wide. I returned the shoes but I had to pay for them—a fruitless and costly experience.

I was busy. There were pupils and lectures. I became accustomed to life in London and waited only for the arrival of my furniture from Vienna to set up a proper home in this immense city.

AN EXPERIMENT IN EDUCATION

I had long wished to study at first-hand, the work of my friend, A. S. Neill, the educational pioneer. I had heard much about Summerhill School, and many members of the staff had been patients of mine, so I was not amidst strangers when I visited the school at a most opportune time—the ending of the school year. At this school the children are left perfectly free. There are neither commands nor prohibitions. The impression produced by these happy youngsters was most remarkable. Mr. and Mrs. Neill were surrounded by a stormy troop of children among whom, however, I

REST IN FOREST (SWITZERLAND)

could not detect a trace of quarreling. This, I am sure, is the result of an education without coercion and bullying. The children seemed to have a mature awareness of responsibilities. Saturday evening is the great occasion when they lodge their complaints at the school meeting. Here, every child over the age of eight has a vote as have the masters and mistresses. Extraordinarily interesting was the theatre, where in addition to a play by Neill, the works of the children were presented. The youngsters, themselves, were the actors, and they also danced and sang, and one could not but look forward to the happier days that are to be expected from "setting the children free."

I had supper with the children. The grown-ups and the young ones have the same food, and any child can ask for a second helping.

At the meeting the punishment is decided by the children, and usually consists of withdrawal of a week's pocket-money, or of permission to attend the cinema.

The place is run on self-government principles, but everything is done to encourage the development of individuality, personal independence, and optimism. My wife was fascinated by what she saw and kept saying: "I cannot but envy these children."

When we think of the discipline in most English schools and that corporal punishment is still administered, we cannot but admire the energy and courage of the Neills and their staff. May the seeds they are sowing thrive. The future of the world depends upon teachers like these, for the world must be rebuilt by a new generation such as this.

Though I do not share Mr. Neill's political views, he and I are good friends, and I wish there were many more idealists such as he.

MEETING OLD FRIENDS

Another visit I paid at about this time was to Norman Haire's country home. At the local station a car was waiting for me, and I enjoyed an agreeable surprise. In the car was a lady, to whom I introduced myself, rightly supposing her to be one of Norman Haire's guests. She answered me in German: "Stekel, you say. Are you Dr. Wilhelm Stekel?"

"Why, yes, who are you?"

"Helene Stöcker." Then I remembered her, though it was years since I had seen her. She had invited me to Berlin, where I lectured before a large audience. She was then in her prime, at the head of the German Women's Movement, and an ardent advocate of the rights of all the oppressed, eager to combat every form of injustice. Each number of her periodical "Die Neue Generation" was a welcome event. During World War I, she would not succumb to the prevalent fanaticism, and became a champion of the movement on behalf of peace and reconciliation. In Nazi Germany the poor woman was therefore treated as a public enemy, had to abandon her beautiful home, leave her library and flee to England.

Barely credible are the experiences of a refugee in London. People whom he has almost completely forgotten cross his path. He meets distinguished persons struggling for subsistence. The uprooted try to get together and mutually search for relief from isolation. Many are thankful to have escaped oppression but cannot endure idleness. They try to keep occupied by learning the new language, and by utilizing other means of killing time.

In London, I was soon surrounded by friends and pupils, old and new. Among them were Neustadter, Maberley, and Samuel Lowy.

THE OUTBREAK OF THE WAR

The war broke out, and I accepted the kind invitation of Mrs. Mundy Castle, a poetess and well-known writer under the name of Whitehouse. Here, I was visited by my friend, John Gunther, who brought me his second book, *Inside Asia,* with a touching autograph inscription, "To the man who gave me Eyes and Wings." Several times he sent me money for which I had not asked, and he offered me further help in case of need.[4]

---

4 John Gunther wrote about Dr. Stekel in LOOK magazine of May 7th, 1940. Speaking about "The Ten Most Interesting People I've Ever Met," he mentioned Archibald MacLeish, Leon Trotzky, Sinclair Lewis, Mahatma Grandhi, Winston Churchill, the Duchess of Windsor, Madame Chiang Kai-Shek, Eamon de Valera, H. G. Wells, and Dr. Wilhelm Stekel. The caption under Stekel's photo is as follows:

"DR. WILHELM STEKEL possesses the most subtle, the most closely packed, the most flashingly intuitive mind I have ever had the good fortune to meet. But Dr. Stekel does not utilize his massive and delicate brain to create new worlds, or to fight wars, or even to write novels. He uses it simply, to mend broken minds and souls.

Dr. Stekel is a Viennese; that is to say, he was not born in Vienna (Viennese, like New Yorkers, are never born there), but he lived in

Freud shared my fate as a refugee. He came to London. I wrote him a letter expressing the wish to bridge our antagonisms in view of the fact that we were both exiles in a foreign land. No answer. I was informed that he was bedridden and did not answer any letters.

EPILOGUE

Here in Tonbridge, in a quiet place, being temporarily without other occupation, I have written this book. My days are spent in composing my autobiography, in weeding the garden, in reading, and sometimes in playing the piano.

If I had the power to relive my life, I should not ask for a different one. I attained a larger measure of success than that of which I dreamed; I have been blessed with love and recognition, and have had better health than most men. My joy of living has been a good companion whatever my situation. I have learned to adapt myself to reality and not to ask for the impossible.

My work in London seems to me like the wish fulfillment in a dream. Sometimes I feel as if I could be grateful to Hitler! I was once invited as a guest of honor to a dinner given by the Royal Astronomic So-

Vienna for a great many years. That also is to say that—in this year of our Lord 1940—he is an exile. When Hitler gobbled up Austria, Dr. Stekel had to flee.

Nowadays, active still and vigorous at 70, he lives in London. For years he was first assistant to Dr. Freud; then he left Freud and founded a school of his own, that of "active" psychotherapy, in contrast to the "passive" school of Freud. (The differences are mostly in technique.) Soon we are to have his autobiography. It should be one of the most stimulating works of our time."—*The Editor.*

ciety Club. I was greeted by the chairman and was
asked to make a speech. Voices called out, "Speak
about Hitler"; other voices, "Speak about miracles."
So in my speech I explained that it was as difficult to
speak about Hitler as about miracles to an astronomical
society which does not believe in miracles. If a year
ago anyone in Vienna had told me, "You will make a
speech before the Royal Astronomic Society Club," I
would have answered, "Only a miracle would produce
it." Hitler worked this miracle.

I had just finished this book when I received the
news of Freud's death. In my writings I have pictured
the pettiness and the foibles of one of the greatest
geniuses of our time, and shown how they influenced
him in relation to myself; but the last thing I want is
to produce the impression that I intended to belittle
the greatness or deny the merits of this singular personality. Nobody would doubt the greatness of Wagner
because his character shows some very mean and unbe-
coming features. His relations to Meyerbeer disclosed
him first as a flatterer and admirer. Later he attacked
Meyerbeer in an article entitled "Judaism in Music"
but who would deny that Wagner in his music reached
an almost incredible height? His operas are written for
eternity, fill thousands and more thousands of hearts
with enthusiasm and lift them out of everyday life.

I told myself that Freud's integral character had only
one goal, to serve the truth, his truth. It was the work
of fate that I could not see my truth through the same
glasses. Posterity will decide the importance of Freud.
He started a new era in psychology by destroying the
old idols of academic science. Innumerable "neurot-

ics" thanked him for guiding them to health. I have every reason for being grateful to him. In spite of all our differences I am dominated by a profound sense of gratitude. I am thankful to fate that I came into touch with this giant. What direction would my life have taken if Kahane had not said, "Come and see Freud?"

I remember that one summer Freud, Adler, and myself had our lodgings in the same neighborhood. Is it an accident that Adler and Freud are buried in English soil, that here, likewise, will probably be my last resting place? Is it not more than a symbol that the leaders of a new science have found in England understanding and refuge? The new psychology driven out from the land of its origin has found in free England protection and understanding and a home. Does it mean that England will maintain the leadership in the freedom of science?

While I write, the war rages, guns are roaring, innocent people are killed by bombs; ships are sunk that were freighted with food for those who are fighting Nazi Germany. The fate of mankind was never decided by wars. Thoughts are stronger than guns. We thank Rousseau and Voltaire for the French Revolution which hoisted the flag of freedom and human dignity. Who knows whether Freud has not inaugurated a similar revolution, and that its ferments will not leaven a new world?

The fact that after the rape of Austria, Freud had to leave the land of his birth will one day be regarded as one of the blackest crimes of the Nazis. I can imagine, nay more, it is my conviction that in days to come his coffin will be brought in triumph to Vienna, and that an immense crowd of mourners will pay him the honor that was denied him during the reign of "the master race." Ideals cannot be destroyed by political movements. Our work will last longer than this epidemic of hatred.

Tranquilly, I look forward to my own demise. I have done my utmost to turn life to account, and life has given me all that any mortal can expect. My autobiography is in substance "my last will and testament."

In the charming book, *A Greek Garland,* translated by my friend, F. L. Lucas, a poet of renown, I have found the following verses of Philodemus. Lucas gave them the title, "Years of Discretion." May these beautiful verses finish my book.

"I have loved but then who has not? Frolicked—who has not tasted
Such frolicks once? Done follies—'tis a god who makes us fools.
Enough! Fast round my temples the dark hair dwindles, wasted
By silver threads, foretelling the years when folly cools.
We played while it was playtime. Now that the season brings
Farewell to that, we'll turn us to think of wiser things."

THE END

INDEX